CHOOSING FORGIVENESS

Your Journey to Freedom

CHOOSING FORGIVENESS

Your Journey to Freedom

NANCY LEIGH DEMOSS

Bestselling author of *Lies Women Believe*

WITH LAWRENCE KIMBROUGH

MOODY PUBLISHERS
CHICAGO

All Scripture quotations, unless otherwise indicated, are taken from the *Holy Bible, English Standard Version*. Copyright © 2000, 2001 by Crossway Bibles, a division of Good News Publishers. Used by permission. All rights reserved.

Scripture quotations marked NASB are taken from the *New American Standard Bible®*, Copyright © 1960, 1962, 1963, 1968, 1971, 1972, 1973, 1975, 1977, 1995 by the Lockman Foundation. Used by permission. (www.Lockman.org)

Scripture quotations marked NIV are taken from the *Holy Bible, New International Version®*. NIV®. Copyright © 1973, 1978, 1984 by International Bible Society. Used by permission of Zondervan Publishing House. All rights reserved.

Scripture quotations marked HCSB are taken from *The Holman Christian Standard Bible* © 2001, Broadman & Holman Publishers, Lifeway Christian Resources, 127 Ninth Avenue North, Nashville, Tennessee 37234. All rights reserved.

Scripture quotations marked NLT are taken from the *Holy Bible, New Living Translation*, copyright © 1996. Used by permission of Tyndale House Publishers, Inc., Wheaton, Illinois, U.S.A. All rights reserved.

Scripture quotations marked NKJV are taken from the *New King James Version*. Copyright © 1982 by Thomas Nelson, Inc. Used by permission. All rights reserved.

Scripture quotations marked KJV are taken from the King James Version.

Emphasis on Scripture citations has been added by the author.

Published in association with the literary agency of Wolgemuth and Associates, Inc

Cover Design: John Hamilton | John Hamilton Design (www.johnhamiltondesign.com)
Cover Image: iStockPhoto
Interior Design: Ragont Design
Editor: Elizabeth Cody Newenhuyse

Library of Congress Cataloging-in-Publication Data
DeMoss, Nancy Leigh.
    Choosing forgiveness : your journey to freedom / Nancy Leigh DeMoss.
       p. cm.
    Includes bibliographical references.
    ISBN-13: 978-0-8024-3253-7
    ISBN-10: 0-8024-3253-0
    1. Forgiveness of sin. 2. Forgiveness—Religious aspects—Christianity. I. Title.
BT795.D46 2006
241'.4—dc22

                                                                    2006022791.

We hope you enjoy this book from Moody Publishers. Our goal is to provide high-quality, thought-provoking books and products that connect truth to your real needs and challenges. For more information on other books and products written and produced from a biblical perspective, go to www.moodypublishers.com or write to:

Moody Publishers
820 N. LaSalle Boulevard
Chicago, IL 60610

3 5 7 9 10 8 6 4

Printed in the United States of America

O GOD
OUR SON'S BLOOD HAS MULTIPLIED THE FRUIT OF
THE SPIRIT IN THE SOIL OF OUR SOULS;
SO WHEN HIS MURDERERS STAND BEFORE THEE
ON THE DAY OF JUDGMENT
REMEMBER THE FRUIT OF THE SPIRIT
BY WHICH THEY HAVE ENRICHED
OUR LIVES. AND FORGIVE.

—*BISHOP HASSAN DEHQANI-TAFTI OF IRAN*[1]

CONTENTS

FOREWORD

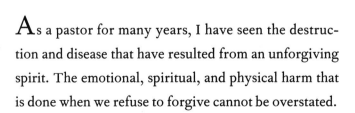

As a pastor for many years, I have seen the destruction and disease that have resulted from an unforgiving spirit. The emotional, spiritual, and physical harm that is done when we refuse to forgive cannot be overstated.

Someone has described unforgiveness as the accumulation of unexpressed anger. Because it is denied, it can often be ignored, while all the time it is building and growing like an invisible tumor. The effort to stuff our hurts below the reach of conscious memory is like trying to hold a fully inflated beach ball under water. The slightest shift in pressure and off it goes, shooting off beyond control.

Psychologists tell us that the weeds of bitterness and unforgiveness are cultivated at great price. When we choose to hold on to our grudges, we relinquish control of our future. We trade the freshness of the new day and all its possibilities for the pain of the past. Quite often, we waste precious mental and spiritual energy brooding over someone who may be far away and totally unaware of our thoughts, or perhaps totally unaware of what happened, and—certainly—totally unaffected by anything we're thinking or doing.

But before you have finished reading the title to this book, you will have absorbed the most important truth about forgiveness. Forgiveness is a choice! Nancy Leigh DeMoss makes it abundantly clear that each of us has the power to forgive and be forgiven.

From real-life stories, we are able to see the joy of forgiveness and the bitterness of prolonged resentment. Each chapter invites you to experience the spiritual and emotional dynamic of forgiveness.

This is an interactive book that asks you important questions. In several places, the author gives you a checklist to help you evaluate your progress in the forgiveness cycle. I found these questions to be practical and penetrating and very self-revealing.

While Nancy Leigh DeMoss is a fine author, she is first of all a Bible teacher. As you would expect from any book with her name on the cover, this book is filled with the exposition of Scripture. I cannot think of one key passage on forgiveness that she overlooked. In a scholarly and practical way, each scriptural text is forcefully unpacked so that the message of forgiveness is clearly understood.

Choosing Forgiveness is missing the platitudes that so frequently find their way into books like this. There are no formulas or simple answers. But if you are looking for the reality and beauty of biblical forgiveness, you will find it here.

Nancy's dealing with the issue of "self-forgiveness" is the best treatment of this question that I have read anywhere. If you happen to be among the many who believe you can be forgiven by God and, at the same time, not forgive yourself, this book will set you free from that bondage.

Whether you need to forgive or be forgiven, you will find the spiritual strength you need between the covers of this book.

DAVID JEREMIAH
Senior Pastor, Shadow Mountain Community Church
President, Turning Point Ministries

WITH
GRATITUDE ...

It hardly seems right to me that my name should appear alone on the cover of any book.

For, as anyone who has written a book—or accomplished any other challenging feat, from building a house to launching a business to growing a family—knows, there are virtually no solo undertakings of any great worth or lasting value.

Each book I write, each message I share with others,

is the fruit of God's gracious work in my life. And my life has been shaped by a host of teachers, mentors, pastors, spiritual leaders, authors, speakers, and friends who have tutored me in His ways, incarnated His truth before my eyes, and poured themselves into my life over the course of nearly five decades. The list of their names (including those whose names I will never know this side of heaven) and the ways they have contributed to my life and ministry could, I would think, fill a book of substantial length.

The Lord knows how deeply indebted I consider myself to be and how very grateful I am for each of these faithful servants.

As it relates to this book in particular, and at the risk of omitting some names that should be included, I gratefully recognize the following for their part in the birthing process:

> ✤ *Lawrence Kimbrough,* who took piles of my notes, message transcripts, files, and e-mails, along with a few phone conversations, and skillfully assembled and shaped the assorted pieces into an initial draft that expressed my heart, and then assisted with the further development of many sections. Lawrence is a gifted writer who is grounded in the Scripture and has a warm heart toward the Lord. His fingerprints are evident throughout this book, which is a better book than I could have written without his considerable efforts and input.

> ✤ *Robert Wolgemuth,* who introduced me to Lawrence and has provided valuable support to me and to the Moody

Publishers team throughout this process.

❋ *My dear friends at Moody Publishers*—including Greg Thornton, Elsa Mazon (now with Moody Broadcasting), Betsey Newenhuyse, Dave DeWit, Judy Tollberg, John Hinkley, and others—who share my passion for seeing lives transformed by the power of His Truth.

❋ *Dr. Bruce Ware* for his careful theological review of not one, but two, versions of the manuscript. He and his wife, Jodi, are kindred spirits and have been a great encouragement to this servant.

❋ *Friends who read the manuscript* at various stages and offered helpful input, including Del Fehsenfeld III, Andrea Griffith, Paula Hendricks, Laine and Janet Johnson, and Kim Wagner, as well as Dawn-Marie Wilson who also provided research assistance. And then there's my precious sister, Elisabeth DeMoss, who keeps me supplied with meaningful illustrations and quotes.

❋ *Mike Neises,* long-time colleague and Director of Publishing for *Revive Our Hearts*—there is no way to measure or adequately recognize the contribution of his wise leadership, oversight, counsel, and handling of issues on a myriad of fronts.

❋ *Sandy Bixel,* my executive assistant extraordinaire, whose servant's heart and administrative gifts make me a far more productive and fruitful servant than I could ever be without her!

❋ *Each of the men and women who serves with me on the staff of Revive Our Hearts*—this incredible team of fellow servants is a rich and undeserved blessing from the Lord. Their encouragement, prayers, and indefatigable labors—way above and beyond the call of duty during a difficult year of transition in our ministry—have made it possible for me to devote the time required to write this book.

❋ *My beloved "Praying Friends," along with scores of others* who labored in the birthing room with me, interceding on my behalf and on behalf of those whose lives would be set free through this call to choose the path of forgiveness.

TO BE FORGIVEN IS SUCH SWEETNESS
THAT HONEY IS TASTELESS IN COMPARISON WITH IT.
BUT YET THERE IS ONE THING
SWEETER STILL AND THAT IS TO FORGIVE.

—*C. H. SPURGEON*

INTRODUCTION

Regina Hockett stood in line at the supermarket checkout, wrapping up a routine transaction on a routine day. Suddenly, she began to sense a disturbance taking place around her, an unusual level of bustle and voices. She felt those first waves of alarm and adrenaline that wash over you when you sense you're in danger.

Instinctively, she turned to make sure her twelve-year-old daughter, Adriane, was at her side—right where she'd been just a moment earlier when she had asked her mom for a quarter to buy something from the gumball machine.

But Adriane was nowhere in sight.

Sometime in those slender moments between then and now, the girl had remembered where her mother kept spare change in the car. She had slipped outside, flipped open the car ashtray to retrieve a quarter, and started making her way back toward the store entrance, intending to exchange the coin for bubble gum.

At that moment, against a crimson mid-October sunset, a lone rifle shot popped in the parking lot. Panic ensued.

By now, Regina was tripping up and down the aisles and cash register lanes, calling Adriane's name, her eyes darting, scanning, flashing. *Where could she be? She was right here!* Finally rushing outside past people in furious motion, she spotted a young girl lying lifeless on the pavement; familiar-looking shoes glinted in the streetlights.

It was Adriane. She was dead.

But why?

It would be three long years before the answer to that question began to emerge, three tearful anniversaries spent wondering who had done this and where they were hiding.

Over time, the facts came to light. Two teenage gang members had set out that night to "make a name" for their renegade group. As they cruised the store parking lot in this middle-class Nashville neighborhood—window down on the passenger side, a sleek assault rifle fully loaded in one lap—they had picked out at random a middle-aged woman standing by her car. *I guess she'll do for a target.*

Something caused the shooter to miss his mark, and the bullet found its way instead into a sixth-grade honor student.

The suspects smiled and laughed at the judge when they were finally apprehended and brought into night court and the charges against them were read. One of them even threatened the detective who accompanied them in, warning him that he'd never live to see their trial date.

As it turned out, this had been just the first of three murders committed by the pair within four months.

You can be sure it was the first time Regina had ever felt pain this deep. "I was broken, broken as could be," she said. "For a year, I was so broken, so depressed I couldn't do anything."

The years rolled by, each one a reminder of what she'd lost, each one a strained effort to imagine what Adriane would be doing, where she'd be going, what she'd be like . . . if she were here.

When Regina spoke out publicly in an October 2005 interview with *The Tennessean* newspaper[1] ten years following the murder, she admitted that she would never fully understand why her precious daughter had to die this way. "But I know this: Adriane's in heaven, and God has given me the power to say something I never thought I could say—'*I forgive.*'"

In fact, her grief had led her to find out as much as she could about the killers who had taken her daughter's life. She learned about their dysfunctional upbringings, their splintered families, their lack of role models.

She even joined an organization that ministered to prisoners on death row. Regina remembers well her first opportunity to visit there one day with a group. While talking with the warden in the hallway, one of the death row prisoners passed nearby, his leg chains clanking, his face where she could see him.

It was Adriane's killer. Right before her eyes. She should have felt anger, she thought. Instead, she felt pity.

"My heart was so heavy, because I had been praying for both of these young men. My prayer is that they come to a place and find God, and know that they don't have to live a miserable life, even there."

Even them.

'How Can I?'

I would like to be able to tell you that forgiveness doesn't require such total surrender and relinquishment. In fact, in a sense, it would be easier to sidestep this subject altogether, because we live in a day when so many are dealing with issues that penetrate to the core of their being, so many for whom holding others at arm's length appears to be the only way to cope.

Unfaithful spouses. Neglectful, insensitive parents. Harsh memories of sexual abuse. Rebellious children. Heartless in-laws. Overbearing bosses and authority figures. I could go on and on.

Through some thirty years of ministry, I have encountered more pain in human hearts and relationships than I would have thought possible.

I don't think I'll ever forget the woman, for example, who stepped to the microphone at a conference where I was speaking and poured out the tragic story of her adult daughter's vicious murder at the hands of a stalker. I can still hear the deep anguish and emotion in this mother's voice, as she stood next to me in front of hundreds of women and cried out, "I've hated this man for fourteen years! How can I forgive? *How can I forgive?*"

I think of another woman, dealing with a much different set of experiences and circumstances, who wrote and said, "I feel like a robot Christian. I've shut God out of my life, and I'm just going through the motions because of all the hurts I've endured."

And the woman who shared, "Last year my father's church threw him out as their pastor. They've sinned against him. They've wronged him. And there are still many broken relationships as a result." Then, expressing both the sense

> *If we are going to be true instruments of mercy in each other's lives, we must deal in truth—* God's *truth.*

of helplessness and the longing she felt in her heart, she asked, *"How do you forgive a whole church?"*

Our hearts ache at the thought of such injustice and pain. When people tell us these kinds of stories, we want to say, "If I were in your shoes, I'd feel the exact same way." Our natural inclination is to wish upon those offenders at least a measure of what they deserve.

But if we are going to be true instruments of mercy in each other's lives, we must deal in truth—*God's* truth. Not blissful, artificial denial, trying to act as though the hurt never happened. Not rigid, mechanical words and formulas, as if following some legalistic, step-by-step recipe were all that was required.

I'm talking about the sweet, rich, pure Word and ways of God, not laid perfunctorily or unnaturally atop our real-life experiences, but pulsing with vitality, healing, and grace, as God wrests reconciliation from the jaws of brokenness; as He restores, redeems, and (ultimately) makes all things new.

His truth is even strong enough to face situations where an apology never comes—or where an apology is impossible due to death or some other restriction—strong enough to leave us free and whole, heart and soul, by the gift of forgiveness.

That's His way of doing things.

The prevailing mind-set in our culture today (and far too often, in the evangelical world as well) leaves us with permission to be coddled, even empowered, in our resentment, our broken relationships, and our unresolved conflicts. Well-meaning friends sometimes come alongside us, supporting our stubborn determination to exact payment from those who have sinned against us, sympathizing with our self-pity.

But the Word of God is clear that the cost of unforgiveness is great. We cannot expect to live at peace with God or to experience His blessing in our lives if we refuse to forgive our debtors. To do so is to choke out His grace and to allow Satan to "get an advantage of us" (2 Corinthians 2:11 KJV).

The wounds that have been inflicted upon you will not be made one ounce lighter by being stored up and left to fester. In fact, they will only become heavier and more burdensome.

Sympathy can provide temporary *relief*, but nothing short of forgiveness can procure lasting *release*.

The Sharp Teeth of Bitterness

One of the most memorable characters in Charles Dickens' classic novel *Great Expectations* is an eccentric old lady named Miss Havisham. By the time we actually meet this unusual person in the story, it is her birthday. Years earlier—on this very calendar day—she had been dressing for her wedding, waiting for her fiancé to arrive. But at twenty minutes till nine, she received the numbing word that her groom had run away with another woman and would therefore not be coming . . . now or ever.

From that moment on, life stopped for Miss Havisham. Every clock in her house was stopped precisely at the fateful hour of twenty minutes till nine. Heavy drapes were hung in the windows, blocking out all sunlight from her dim and ever more dingy home. She lived in seclusion with her adopted daughter, Estella, while the wedding cake and feast lay rotting on the table, spiders carrying them off in bits and pieces, and mice scurried audibly in the walls.

Most vivid of all, the jilted bride-to-be continued to wear the now-fragile dress and wedding veil she had been wearing at the moment of her tragedy, their colors long since faded and yellowed, their lace and fabric in tatters.

To the main character, Pip, who has arrived at her house through his attraction to Estella and naturally wonders why this spectacle is taking place—(*wouldn't you?*)—Miss Havisham gives this depressing analysis: "On this day of the year, long before you were born, this heap of decay . . . was brought here. It and I have worn away together. The mice have gnawed at it, and *sharper teeth than teeth of mice have gnawed at me*" (emphasis added).[2]

Forgiveness is not a method to be learned as much as a truth to be lived.

Those "teeth" were (and are) the sharp edges of bitterness, resentment, and unforgiveness. Tearing deeper than the flesh wounds of claw and fang, these knifelike protrusions can pierce far beneath the skin, eating away at joy, eroding peace, and closing our hearts off to the sunlight of God's presence.

Oh, our plight may not be as obviously pathetic as that of Miss Havisham. We may find ways to numb ourselves to the pain, to carry on in spite of our resentment, even, perhaps, to maintain a semblance of normalcy. But our inner spirit bears the telltale signs of those gnawing teeth and of the darkened room in which we have chosen to live.

Has the clock stopped in *your* life? Was there a moment when someone or something hurt you—and everything changed? Perhaps you can still remember the day, the time, the year, the scenery, the circumstances. Your hopes, dreams, and innocence felt the sharp sting of betrayal and disappointment. Ever since, the story of your life has been to recapture your loss and seek your revenge, either through outright action or the withholding of love and affection.

Do you know full well what those gnawing teeth feel like?

I want to say to you that you don't have to live there. It's time to pull back the drapes and move out of the darkness. To do so may seem risky—even impossible. The process may be painful. But there is life and health and a whole new world outside the dark, musty walls of hurt and disillusionment behind which you have barricaded your heart. God wants to give you the grace to move on . . . He wants to set you free.

A Truth to Be Lived

Throughout this book we'll be looking at what forgiveness is and what it isn't, exploring it in the light of the Scripture, delving into its promises while debunking some of its myths. We'll talk specifically about how we go about doing it, how we actually put God's grace and mercy into practice, as He has done with us.

But nowhere in the best of principles and insights I can offer, nowhere in the Scripture, will we come upon a magic word or a secret formula. Forgiveness is not a method to be learned as much as a truth to be lived. The concept of forgiveness will hardly be foreign to most who read this book. It's unlikely that you will discover many, if any, profound new insights in these pages.

For most of us, the problem isn't that we don't know about forgiveness. The problem, as I've witnessed it in one life after another (including my own far too often), is either that we haven't recognized and acknowledged the unforgiveness that's in our hearts, or that we simply haven't made the choice to forgive.

In urging you to choose the pathway of forgiveness, with all its risks and difficulties, I don't intend to imply that what has happened to you isn't as bad as you're making it out to be. What you have suffered is real.

You may have endured unspeakably evil treatment at the hands of a close relative—or a trusted friend or a complete stranger. There may be tender areas of your life that can hardly bear to be touched, due to past—or present—circumstances that you still cannot bring yourself to share with another.

I don't want to belittle or minimize the experiences that have made a painful imprint on your soul. In fact, though some may insist you need to "forgive and forget," the truth is, forgiveness at its best requires that you face how badly you've been hurt.

But along the way, we will discover this hard yet healing truth: whatever sin has been committed against you, the choice not to forgive is itself a serious sin. In fact, failing to forgive can often bring about problems in your life far worse and more long-term than the pain of the original offense.

My Prayer for You

I have felt compelled to write this book—because I know that most believers are faced with the ripple effects of unforgiveness every day in some form or another. It affects men and women, old and young, married and single, wealthy and poor.

It can be a response to unspeakable offenses, some of which may span decades, or to passing insults and injuries that seem microscopic by comparison but hurt nonetheless.

I have seen unforgiveness wreak havoc on marriages and churches and workplaces and ministries; I have seen it destroy long-time friendships.

John MacArthur's long experience as a pastor has convinced him that "nearly all the personal problems that drive people to seek pastoral counsel are related in some way to the issue of forgiveness."[3] Simply said, this is a *huge* issue.

Even as you read these words, resentment may be a raging fire within you. Or it may be less intense—more like a dull ache. It may have become so familiar and habitual that you can't remember what it was like to ever live without it. Or it may be so subtle and disguised that you don't even recognize it for what it is. Regardless, you don't have to go on that way. The choice to forgive will set you on a journey to freedom.

"See to it," the writer of Hebrews said, "that no one fails to obtain the grace of God; that no 'root of bitterness' springs up and causes trouble, and by it many become defiled" (Hebrews 12:15).

See to it. Those are the inspired words of God that drive me into waters where I know I run the risk of being perceived as insensitive or simplistic, of sounding cold and calloused. My earnest prayer is that every person who reads these words will "obtain the grace of God"—and that you will release every hostage you may be holding in the prison of your mind and emotions . . . and in so doing find yourself released as well.

This is God's plan for you. This is God's best for you. And this is God's will for you.

Forgiveness.

WE TALK GLIBLY ABOUT FORGIVING
WHEN WE HAVE NEVER BEEN INJURED;
WHEN WE ARE INJURED WE KNOW
THAT IT IS NOT POSSIBLE, APART FROM GOD'S GRACE,
FOR ONE HUMAN BEING TO FORGIVE ANOTHER.

—*OSWALD CHAMBERS*

WALKING WOUNDED

A friend told me as I was working on this book, "I
don't really relate to this subject—I just don't struggle
with bitterness or unforgiveness."

While that may be true for a few, I've come to believe that, whether they realize it or not, unforgiveness
is, in fact, a very real issue for *most* people. Almost
everyone has someone (or ones) they haven't forgiven.

I've seen it confirmed over and over again. For

many years, whenever I have spoken on this subject, after defining and describing forgiveness from a biblical perspective, I have asked the audience this question: "How many of you would be honest enough to admit that there is a root of bitterness in your heart—that there are one or more people in your life—past or present—that you've never forgiven?"

I have asked for a response from tens of thousands of people, including long-time believers, Bible study leaders, and vocational Christian workers. It doesn't matter what the setting is or who's in the audience. In virtually every case, somewhere between 80 and 95 percent of the hands in the room have been raised.

It still affects me profoundly to think that the vast majority of people sitting in church Sunday after Sunday (and many who are sitting at home, having left the church, disillusioned) have at least a seed—if not a forest—of unforgiveness in their heart.

In many cases, those raised hands reveal hearts that are still wounded, still bleeding, still suffering, still hearing the words, still seeing the offenses, still having a hard time getting over what happened.

In other cases, the hands represent hearts that have been anesthetized; they have become indifferent or detached, perhaps putting up walls to keep from getting hurt again.

Whatever the story behind each hand raised, I am convinced that unforgiveness in the hearts of God's people is not the exception—it has become the *norm* for most. They may have learned to live with it. They may be "coping." They may mask it with laughter or bury it with busyness. But when they get honest with themselves and God, they are not free.

So while I'm well aware that there are other good books and resources available on this subject . . . I keep seeing that sea of raised hands. People just like you. I keep thinking of the eyes I've looked into and the stories I've heard from tormented—or jaded—hearts. More important, I keep thinking about how different people's lives can be once the walls are broken down, once they choose the pathway of forgiveness and are set free from the prison of hurt and bitterness.

Deep Slices of Life

We can't talk about forgiveness without acknowledging the reality of pain. If we were never hurt, there would be no need for forgiveness.

Truly, we are a generation of wounded people. And wounded people tend to wound other people. (You may have heard it said that the most dangerous animal in the forest is the one that's been wounded.) Just look around at all the random violence and dysfunction. Road rage. Kids walking into schools with guns and blowing people's heads off. Where does it all come from? More often than not, it is the result of harbored hurt and smoldering bitterness that has turned to anger, hatred, revenge, and violence.

When I speak of hurt, what comes to your mind?

You may have been forced to endure a childhood of sexual

abuse. Perhaps it was a brother, a relative, maybe your own father who used you to meet some twisted, missing need in his own heart. Perhaps the fallout led you into a life of promiscuity that even now haunts you with anger, guilt, and regret.

Maybe the abuse wasn't as much physical as it was emotional and manipulative. Perhaps the dysfunction in your home played itself out in ways that have complicated and convoluted nearly all your relationships ever since, and you've never stopped blaming your mom or your dad or your grandparents—somebody!—for giving you such a poor start to life.

It could be a husband who is habitually distant and inexpressive, a mate whose priorities have never really been on the same page as yours, who regularly forgets or ignores things that matter to you.

Is the ugly residue of hurt just your lot in life? And would you really believe it if the answer was no?

It could be a sister or brother who's quibbled with you over both important and petty family matters. It's made your adult relationship with that sibling strained and superficial, turning almost every holiday or family gathering into an

awkward chore, another opportunity for taking sides and enduring insults.

Perhaps it's a new management player in the company you
work for who has made you feel unvalued and marginalized.
Perhaps it's a son-in-law who's brought pain into your daughter's life or has poisoned your relationship with your grandchildren. Or a pastor who broke trust with your whole fellowship
by entering into an adulterous affair, making your church more
soap opera than sanctuary. Or perhaps it's a woman who lured
your husband away from you, and now your anger and resentment toward both of them has infected your thoughts, your attitudes, and your daily routine.

Or if it's none of these . . . it's something. Someone. Some
situation that rears its head with painful frequency and brings all
the emotions flooding back in like a torrent.

It's left you with a heart that often feels like it's tied up in
knots. It seems like you're constantly at war, always on guard
against an onslaught of conflicting feelings.

It's interrupted the free flow of worship and sweetness you
used to experience in your relationship with God. You miss it.
You miss Him. It's like going around each day with a low-grade
fever—if not a dangerously high one! It's changed everything
the word "normal" used to mean in your life.

The question is: *Do those wounds—past or present—have to
define who you are, where you're headed, and how you get there?* Is
the ugly residue of hurt just your lot in life?

And would you really believe it if the answer was no?

If You Only Knew

Matters that require forgiveness tend to hit us right where we live. They rarely play fair and can come with little or no warning. And though they may be similar to what others have experienced, they often raise their own set of tough questions.

For example:

What do you do when the problem is not simply an old wound from the past but one that's continually being opened and re-injured? How do you handle it when the activity that led you into your current state of anger and bitterness isn't a distant memory but rather an ongoing occurrence (as a friend asked me just yesterday)?

Or how do you simultaneously forgive someone while also bearing the responsibility of protecting yourself—perhaps even your children—from the danger this person poses to you?

How do you deal with the sights and sounds, the flashbacks that crop up out of nowhere, the markers and anniversaries that continually roll around or unsheathe themselves at random times of day?

What about when your anger is focused not against a person who did something to *you* but against someone who has harmed a person you love? Should it not bring out the mother bear in you when your son is bullied at school, or your daughter is mistreated by other girls, or your husband is backstabbed by an unscrupulous co-worker?

What about the guy who talked of marriage, who seemed

like the man God wanted in your life, but in the end he walked away, playing lightly with your heart? How do you deal with the damage he left in his wake?

Where do you even begin to forgive your wife, who's seemed to have become a whole other person in the past year, who's giving you every indication that she's enjoying the advances of another man and doesn't really seem to care what you think about it?

How do you respond to the person who writes,

Trouble has come upon my family. Where there should be love there is hatred, and where there should be compassion there is sorrow and fighting and arguing.

Or this one:

Please, please pray for my family. I am at the end of my rope with all the anger and unforgiveness and hatred in my family.

Truly, these are God-sized wounds that need God-sized answers. No formulaic words, no wave of a wand will put things back like they were. We can't press the "UNDO" button and hope to see our lives returned to the way we once knew them or the way we hoped they would turn out.

When the pain is this close, when the wound is this tender, when the offense is this obvious, how do we forgive?

Painful Realities

I want to begin sorting through these questions by just letting this one expectation settle in around us, as basic and obvious
as it may seem:

Everyone will get hurt.

It's a fact of life. Pain is unavoidable in this fallen world.
You *will* be hurt, wronged, and offended by others. There's no
way around it.

"In this world you will have trouble," Jesus assured His anx-
ious, bewildered followers (John 16:33 NIV), much as Paul
would remind his young charge, Timothy, at a later time: "Indeed, all who desire to live a godly life in Christ Jesus will be
persecuted" (2 Timothy 3:12). So the issue is not whether we're
being particularly godly or not. For while obedience does bring
its share of eternal blessing, it is equally true that problems and
pain can and will rain down on the best of us—sometimes harder
on Christians than others.

True, one person's experiences will differ from another's by
specifics and degree. Some will experience pain that's far worse
than that of others. But the fact remains universal that all of us
will suffer harm of some kind . . . likely many times along the way.
We will all encounter situations that provide fertile ground for resentment and unforgiveness to take root and bloom in our hearts.

That much is obvious. No disagreement there. But I want to
challenge you to consider another observation that may not be
quite so easy to accept:

*The outcome of our lives is not determined by what happens to us
but by how we respond to what happens to us.*

Did you get that? The outcome of your life and mine—who
we are, how we function, our personal well-being, our future, our
relationships, our usefulness—none of that is ultimately determined by anything that anyone has done or could do to hurt us.

Of course, we will be *affected* by the circumstances that form
the backdrop of our lives. They will carve grooves into our
hearts that will always be part of our experience. But those circumstances, horrendous as they may be, do not have the power
to *control* the outcome of our lives.

As long as we believe
that our happiness and
well-being are determined
by what happens to us,
we will always be *victims*,
because so much of what
happens to us is beyond
our control. There's no
possibility of hope in that
perspective—we can never
be different, never be
whole, never be free. To
greater or lesser degrees
(depending on how we
have been treated or

*Our only hope lies
in realizing that we
do have a choice
about how we
respond to life's
circumstances.*

mistreated) we will always be damaged goods, destined to be dysfunctional people in a dysfunctional world.

We simply don't have any choice about many of the things that happen to us. Our only hope lies in realizing that we *do* have a choice about how we *respond* to life's circumstances—and it is those responses that determine the outcome of our lives.

Now that may not sound like good news to you. "You're telling me that *I'm* responsible? That puts the burden back on *me*—what kind of encouragement is that?"

But to whatever extent you may have been imprisoned by your response to wounds inflicted on you by others, I assure you that embracing this truth is the starting place in your journey to freedom.

When we as God's children realize that His grace is sufficient for every situation, that by the power of His indwelling Spirit we have the ability to respond with grace and forgiveness to those who have sinned against us—at that point we are no longer victims. We are free to rise above whatever may have been done to us, to grow through it, and to become instruments of grace, reconciliation, and redemption in the lives of other hurting people and even in the lives of our offenders.

Yes, we can be free—if we choose to be.

Keeping Count

There are essentially two ways of responding to life's hurts and unfair experiences. Every time we get hurt, we choose to respond in one of these two ways.

The first, natural response is to become a *debt collector*. We set out to make the offender pay for what he has done. We may be overt or subtle, but until we get a satisfactory apology, until we determine that an adequate penalty has been paid, we intend on keeping the wrongdoer in debtors' prison; we reserve the right to punish them for their transgression. This is the pathway of resentment and retaliation—getting even, exacting payment for what they did.

Instead of releasing our grip on the offenses we've received and letting God be the one (the *only* one) who's big and strong enough to handle the problem in His perfect, just, and redemptive way, we grab hold of the hurt and refuse to let it go. We hold our offender hostage (we think).

Think Esau and Jacob. A birthright deceptively stolen. The lifelong expectation of opportunity and prosperity finally within Esau's grasp, but now—by a trick, a conspiracy worked up by a mother playing favorites—Esau's rightful pathway to a father's blessing is wildly derailed at the last minute.

"*So Esau bore a grudge* against Jacob because of the blessing with which his father had blessed him; and Esau said to himself, 'The days of mourning for my father are near; then I will kill my brother Jacob'" (Genesis 27:41 NASB). He was storing it up, biding his time, intent on getting his revenge . . . and then some.

But the problem is that being a "debt collector" does more than keep our offender in debtors' prison; it puts *us* in prison.

A colleague passed on to me a heartrending story he had heard a woman share with her church family, as the Lord was revealing her need to choose the pathway of forgiveness. As a young girl, she and a little friend of hers in their small town went out one day to see the county sheriff, whose office happened to be in the same building as the town jail. The children had always considered the man to be their friend, the nice person with the uniform and the badge who was just fun to be around.

At some point in the afternoon, her girlfriend ran off to play, leaving her alone with the sheriff in his office. Suddenly, the look on his face began making her uncomfortable. The feel of the room became strangely tense and frightening. He moved close to her and whisperingly said, "If you ever tell your parents what I'm about to do to you"—pointing to the iron bars behind him—"I'll put you in one of those jail cells."

And with that, he proceeded to molest her.

The events of that day had occurred many years in the past by the time, as a grown woman, she finally told the story of how the man she thought was a trusted friend had shattered her childhood innocence. Thinking back to what the sheriff had said about locking her up if she were to report him to her mom or dad, she said, "I realize now that in my heart I put *him* in a 'jail cell' that day, and all these years I've kept him in that prison."

When God finally opened her eyes to see what unforgiveness was actually doing to her (and to her marriage), she realized something else: on that day so many years ago, she had put *herself* in jail as well. And though the man was now long dead, unforgiveness and bitterness had kept her locked there—in a cell of her own making—for all those years.

Was it her fault for being taken advantage of by an authority figure? Of course not. That cannot be said strongly enough. But who had been hurt the most by her unforgiveness? And why should she be in "jail" for a crime someone else had committed?

Debt collecting is the natural response of sinful humans to being harmed, abused, or mistreated. Invariably it produces the bitter fruit of deeper pain, resentment, and bondage.

But there is another way. A better way. God's way.

Letting Go

As an alternative to being debt collectors—the pathway of resentment and retaliation—God calls us to the pure, powerful choice of forgiveness—and to pursue, wherever possible, the pathway of restoration and reconciliation.

Actually, this is not presented in Scripture as an option. "As the Lord has forgiven you," Paul writes in Colossians 3:13, "so you also must forgive." There's not a lot of grey area or wiggle room in there.

The Lord Himself was equally clear and direct: "Whenever you stand praying, if you have anything against anyone, forgive him" (Mark 11:25 NKJV). "*Anything* against *anyone.*" That pretty much covers the bases, doesn't it! No offense is too great, no offender is beyond the boundary to which our forgiveness must extend. Our fellowship with God requires it and depends on it.

So if we as believers persist in unforgiveness, our hearts are forced to wrestle with the fact that our actions amount to disobedience. Forgiveness is not a take-or-leave option that only a super-Christian should be expected to take.

Yes, it's unnatural. It's supernatural. At times it's almost unbelievable.

Ask the surgeon whose medical mistake cost my friend Margaret Ashmore's mother her life. She had been rushed to the hospital with chest pains, yet was still visibly bright and alert when tests revealed that she had indeed suffered a mild heart attack. After a quick evaluation among a small group of doctors on staff, it was decided that an angioplasty procedure would be the best route for opening up the perceived blockage in her arteries.

She was immediately wheeled into surgery. Everyone expected her to be fine.

But sometime during the operation, the doctor inflated the balloon apparatus too quickly, too early. Her damaged heart began to fail irreparably, and she sank into a coma.

She died three hours later.

Margaret's father was inconsolable. His wife of forty-two years—a marriage he had treasured with an intense love and loyalty greater than most—had been taken from him in a matter of moments for no good reason because of a surgeon's goof-up.

The days that followed were almost too painful for Margaret to bear. Her kind, gentle father was transforming into a cyclone of anger, grief, despair . . . revenge! Unrelenting in his rage, tormented by his broken heart, he declared himself on a mission to "bring down that hospital!" Demanding a meeting with the hospital administration and the doctors responsible for his wife's care, he vowed to face them and tell them that he was suing them all for everything they had . . . and living to see them suffer.

As the hospital staff and physicians anxiously awaited the arrival of Margaret's dad for the confrontation, they trembled at the thought of what they expected to hear. How does someone in their shoes handle a situation like this?

You don't . . . when God does.

On his way to the meeting, Margaret's dad began to realize that if he ever wanted to be free from this dungeon of anger and bitterness in which he found himself, he would have to do what God had done for him. He would have to forgive.

To the amazement of everyone in the room, as he walked through the door that day, he walked directly over to the man whose misjudgment had ended his dear one's life, extended his hand to him, and said, "The only way I'm going to be able to live with any peace the remainder of my life is to forgive you."

The people in the room sat stunned. The doctor began to weep. For what seemed like forever, he couldn't even let go of the hand of the man who had relinquished his right to retaliate.

Two people walked out of that conference room as free men that day—but none more free than the one who offered the release, the one who did the forgiving.

Like Drinking Poison

Again, nothing about forgiveness is easy. There's no question about that. It's hard to think about. It's hard to do. It's hard to keep doing. But if we could somehow back away from our own situation long enough, out where we could see it more clearly, where the wounds and the scars didn't hurt us every time we turned a certain way or made a sudden movement, we'd see something else.

We'd see that not forgiving only makes it worse.

Rudy Tomjanovich was a four-time NBA All-Star who appeared to be off to another award-winning season in 1977. This was supposed to be the year when his Houston Rockets team was poised to make a run at the title.

On the night of December 9, the Rockets were at the Forum in Los Angeles to play the hometown Lakers. The score was tied, and the second half was just beginning when a scuffle occurred between two of the players near midcourt. Tomjanovich, who was some distance away from the fighting when he first noticed it, began running at a full sprint to come to his teammate's defense.

One of the players involved in the fight, Kermit Washington, remembers catching sight of a quick, red blur out of the corner of his eye—Tomjanovich's red jersey—coming up fast behind him. Wheeling around, he pile-drove his fist into Rudy's face, sending him sprawling backward, the back of his head hitting hard against the floor.

In what has now become known to avid basketball fans as merely "the punch," Tomjanovich lay motionless for several seconds, totally knocked out. In fact, the combination of the swing catching Rudy in full forward motion was likened by doctors to a pair of locomotives colliding at top speed. His injuries resembled those of a person smashing into a windshield at 50 mph.

This wasn't just a bloody nose. (In fact, his wife gets upset even today when someone refers to her husband's injury as a broken nose. "The only thing on his face that *wasn't* broken," she says, "was his nose.") His entire skull had been knocked out of line. His jaws no longer fit together correctly. Even his tear ducts had collapsed.

He had almost been killed.

The next season—five reconstructive surgeries later—Rudy tried to come back and play the game he loved. But only briefly did he rise to the level of performance he had attained before the split-second events of that single night. He retired shortly thereafter, realizing his skills had been compromised, not wanting to relocate his family to another city just to try extending his playing days a little while longer.

It had happened so fast, with hardly any

> ONE DEFINITION OF UNFORGIVENESS:
>
> *"Like drinking poison and hoping someone else would die."*

warning. One day, his idea of "normal" had been the competitive life of a professional athlete. The next, it meant lying for hours in an ICU ward, not sure if he would live or die.

What put him there wasn't really intentional. Something sparked, one thing led to another, a situation just spun out of control. It happens like that sometimes, doesn't it? You can probably think of an event in your own life when things got heated, the pot began to boil over, and the next thing you knew . . . the damage had been done. There was no going back. The things that were said, the things that occurred—they forever changed your life.

But when asked if he had forgiven Kermit Washington for the punch that ruined his playing career, Rudy responded, "Someone once told me that hating Kermit would be like taking poison and hoping someone else would die. I've always tried to remember that."[1]

Like drinking poison and hoping someone else would die. That's a powerful word picture for what unforgiveness is like in the human heart. Though it may feel right, though it may seem justified, though it may appear to be the only option available to us, it is destructive and deadly to the one who drinks it. The very weapon we use to inflict pain on our offender becomes a sword turned inward on ourselves, doing far more damage to us—and to those who love us—than to those who have hurt us.

Finding Freedom

I realize that this journey into forgiveness may require you to delve into areas of your life that are sensitive and still hot to the touch. But I am also aware that our natural way of handling these hurts only results in keeping them sore and inflamed.

It is God's way—and His way alone—that holds out any hope of healing and rescue from the inevitable troubles of life that we face.

It was no idle promise or wishful thinking for Jesus to say, "You will know the truth, and the truth will set you free" (John 8:32). To choose forgiveness and to walk in His truth is God's prescribed pathway—your journey to freedom.

And only those who walk it will find out.

Making It Personal

❋ Is there a person or circumstance you have blamed for the
way your life has turned out? How could accepting responsibility for your response to that person or situation set you
free?

❋ Is there someone who has wronged you that you're still trying
to make pay for their offense? How have you tried to exact
payment from them? What is holding you back from forgiving
that person, releasing them from their debt?

❋ Can you think of a situation where you retaliated or became
resentful, rather than forgiving someone who hurt you? What
were the results? How was your relationship with that person
affected? How did your response change you? How did it affect your relationship with God?

ALL REVENGE IS OF THE NATURE OF POISON,
AND THOUGH WE DON'T TAKE
SO MUCH AS TO PUT AN END TO LIFE,
YET IF WE TAKE ANY AT ALL,
IT CORRUPTS THE WHOLE MASS OF BLOOD
AND MAKES IT DIFFICULT TO
BE RESTORED TO OUR FORMER HEALTH.

—*WILLIAM LAW*

CHAPTER TWO

WHAT HAPPENS WHEN WE REFUSE

W ounded hearts can experience powerful emotions. A heart-wrenching letter sent to our ministry from a boy turned man turned church deacon vividly illustrates how intense those emotions can be and the long-lasting, far-reaching effects they can have over time. It also shows the extraordinary lengths wounded people will sometimes go to in an effort to deal with the pain.

My daddy left us when I was two. I wanted a daddy so bad. I hated him for leaving me. I hated him so much, I wanted him to die and go to hell.

I grew up in the mountains. There is a lot of superstition in the mountains. They said if you drove a nail in a tree and spoke the name of a person while driving the nail that person would die.

There was a big pine tree near where I grew up. I went to that pine tree day after day driving nails and speaking the name of my daddy. I do not know how many nails I drove in that tree, but my daddy did not die. I hated him so much.

The hatred I carried for my daddy wrecked my first marriage, and is threatening my second. I am a shell of a person; I do not have any close personal relationships.

Our society has become so riddled with rancor and bitterness we almost consider it a normal response to life.

As I've worked on this book, I've carried a great burden for readers who resemble the man who wrote that letter. Hatred and bitterness are destroying their lives and relationships—and they know it. But for whatever reason they've never been willing, or felt able, to release that bitterness and forgive their offenders.

I've also been burdened for another group that I suspect is much larger—those who don't think of themselves as bitter, unforgiving people. They aren't hammering nails into trees wishing people dead—but if they would let the Spirit of God open them up, they would discover seeds of bitterness that have taken root in their hearts.

In our therapeutic culture, it's widely acceptable to acknowledge that we've been "hurt" or "wounded"—words that focus on the wrong that has been done to us. But it's a lot harder to admit that we've let that hurt escalate (or *descend*, to use a better word) into unforgiveness or bitterness—which puts responsibility on our shoulders.

Our society has become so riddled with rancor and bitterness we almost consider it a normal response to life. Every day in America, tens of thousands of new lawsuits are filed—millions a year! And those who don't let their bitterness lead them into litigation or erupt into violent crimes and addictions are often saddled with more subtle forms of expression: silent distrust, insecurity, illogical fears, sullen indifference, compulsive agitation and restlessness.

How can you know if hurt has turned to bitterness in your life? You may be like the young Georgia woman who wrote to tell me about the bitterness she had finally come to grips with in her heart over her parents' divorce. "People have always told me," she said, "how 'sweet' I am and that I'm always smiling. But I think deep down I've been bitter and angry about a lot of things. And now that I see it, I want it out of me."

But often we can't see it, even when it's there. How can you tell? For starters, see if you relate to any of these statements:

❊ I often replay in my mind the incident(s) that hurt me.

❊ When I think of a particular person or situation, I still feel angry.

❊ I try hard not to think about the person, event, or circumstance that caused me so much pain.

❊ I have a subtle, secret desire to see this person pay for what he or she did to me.

❊ Deep in my heart, I wouldn't mind if something bad happened to the person(s) who hurt me.

❊ I often find myself telling others how this person has hurt me.

❊ A lot of my conversations revolve around this situation.

❊ Whenever his or her name comes up, I am more likely to say something negative than something positive about him or her.

These kinds of thoughts reveal pockets of resentment and unforgiveness in our hearts. They allow us to see something in ourselves we never thought we'd become.

How Bad Is It?

My intention is not to load you down with guilt or insert additional blame into a situation that's already charged with hurt and emotion. But if we want to be free, we first have to acknowledge the depths that unforgiveness has reached in our lives; we have to recognize the damage it's caused—and *can* cause. And we have to deal with the fact that our unforgiveness is a sin, just as the original offense was. No *worse* of a sin, but certainly no less of one.

Most of us know from experience that when sin of any kind is given a chance to take up residence in our hearts, it doesn't stay confined to its own little corner. If not confessed and repented of, sooner or later it will affect our entire person—our physical and emotional well-being, our demeanor, our whole outlook.

And unforgiveness is no different. When we fail to deal with hurts God's way, when we harbor resentment in our hearts, that bitterness—like an infection—will fester and work its way into our system, until ultimately we start viewing everything through the eyes of hurt—everything others do, everything that happens to us.

So as I try to bring God's Word to bear on this subject and on the painful circumstances you may have experienced, my desire is not to add to your burden but to spare you more pain. I long for you to enjoy the blessing, the freedom, and the transformational power of walking in obedience.

Now, let's explore further what bitterness really is, what it can do, and—more important—begin to discover how it can be overcome by the power and grace of our great God.

A Taste of Bitterness

Most of us are familiar with the apostle Paul's exhortation in Ephesians chapter 4: "Let all bitterness and wrath and anger and clamor and slander be put away from you, along with all malice" (v. 31). We'll take a look later at the other side of the coin as expressed in the following verse ("Be kind to one another, tenderhearted, forgiving one another"). But first, let's focus on what it is we're to get rid of.

The Greek word translated "bitterness" in the New Testament comes from the root word *pik*. It sounds like what it means—the word literally means to prick or cut. It can refer to a sharp or pointed object or to a bitter, sharp taste. Used figuratively, it describes "that angry and resentful state of mind that can develop when we undergo troubles."[1]

Now look again at the other words Paul includes in this list—at the kinds of actions and attitudes that invariably orbit around bitterness:

❋ *Wrath* and *anger*—intensifying degrees of resentment, hostility, and rage that, given the right amount of prodding or pressure, can quickly overflow its banks like a flash flood in a summer storm.

❧ *Clamor* and *slander* (or *evil speaking*)—outbursts of anger out of control; using words to retaliate, to demean, to paint others in a negative light, to wish for them an ill reputation.

❧ *Malice*—a deliberate desire to inflict pain, a premeditated strike at the weak spot in our offender, acting out the bitter thoughts and feelings of our hearts.

Have any of these found a dwelling place in the soil of your heart?

Bitterness in our hearts will inevitably find its way into our speech and our tone of voice. See, for example, how closely "bitterness" and "cursing" appear together in Romans 3:14— "Their mouth is full of curses and bitterness." Both of these are cut from the same ugly cloth.

In Colossians 3:19, Paul contrasts love with bitterness, and warns against letting bitterness infect the marriage relationship: "Husbands, love your wives," he instructs, "and do not be bitter toward them" (NKJV). Other translations say, "Do not be *harsh* with them."

Those two ideas—bitterness and harshness—are tightly linked, even in marriage. I have seen bitterness erode and sabotage more than one marriage. Couples who were once tender and affectionate toward one another end up becoming archenemies, slinging harsh, biting words at one another, returning tit for tat, wound for wound.

So why do we do it? Why do we allow these unwanted intruders —bitterness, anger, malice, harshness, evil speaking—

to move in with us and take up residence, to be kept like harmful poisons in our kitchen cabinets? Just think of it:

❋ Bitterness grieves the Spirit of God.

❋ Such a spirit makes us hard and cold and difficult to live with.

❋ It turns us into people who are negative and critical.

❋ It makes us resistant to God's plan and His love for us.

❋ Eventually it destroys us, the way acid eats through the container in which it's held.

Inviting Torment

You may be thinking at this point, "But you don't understand my situation—it's just not that cut and dried."

Yes, your situation may be much different from those of others you know or those you'll read about in this book. But there are some universal consequences that result from refusing to forgive, no matter how big or small the offense, no matter how tangled or complex the issue.

In that probing parable of the unforgiving servant in Matthew 18, which Jesus told in response to Peter's question, "Lord, how often shall my brother sin against me, and I forgive him? Up to seven times?" (v. 21 NKJV) we see the awful result of harboring grudges against others, in light of how much God has forgiven us.

You know the story. A king discovered that one of his servants owed him "ten thousand talents." One "talent" was equal to about twenty years worth of wages for a normal laborer—so 10,000 talents would be *200,000 years' wages.* If we just use a simple figure of $30,000 as being a fair annual salary, 10,000 talents would be some *$6 billion,* a debt that could not possibly be repaid in many lifetimes!

To put that amount in perspective, in those days the total revenue collected by the Roman government each year from the entire land of Palestine averaged about 900 talents, nowhere near 10,000! Jesus chose this astronomical figure deliberately, intending to represent an unfathomable amount.

The king ordered that the man be brought before him, demanding that he and his family be sold in hopes of recouping at least some of the debt. The servant fell to his knees, begging the king to be patient with him, assuring him (as if he really could) that he would repay him every penny he owed. Even though the king knew the man could never hope to amass such an enormous amount of money, he took pity on

Anytime I hold a grudge, I am like the man who grabbed his debtor by the throat, demanding, "Pay back what you owe me."

him. He canceled the debt. He let him go.

But the plot thickens. For when this servant returned home a forgiven man, he went out looking for one of his fellow servants who owed him "a hundred denarii, and seizing him, he began to choke him, saying, 'Pay what you owe'" (v. 28).

You may have heard "a hundred denarii" equated to no more than a few bucks, mere pocket change. But a single denarius represented a day's wage for a common laborer, so a hundred denarii cashed out at around three months' earnings.

If we use again our assumption of a $30,000 annual salary, this man would have been out around $10,000—no small amount for most workers! So we might find ourselves sympathizing with this servant's response to his debtor—if it weren't for the fact that what was owed him was *nothing* in comparison to the enormous debt he had just been forgiven.

When I read what the forgiven servant did to his fellow servant, I can feel my blood pressure begin to rise. I find his cold-heartedness and ingratitude incredulous. But it's right about that time that I sense the Holy Spirit gently pointing His finger at my own heart, saying, "Isn't that what you do?"

Every time I refuse to forgive, anytime I hold a grudge, I am like the man who grabbed his debtor by the throat, demanding, "Pay back what you owe me."

When hauled back before the king who had canceled his impossible debt, this man was handed over to "tormentors" (v. 34 kjv)—"jailers," the English Standard Version says—until he paid back everything he owed.

"Jailers." Isn't that telling in light of the last chapter, when we think of the prison we find ourselves in by virtue of our unforgiveness?

The man who had his debtor thrown into prison ended up in debtors' prison himself, being tormented in the very way he had treated his debtor.

In case we've managed to miss it, Jesus makes the main point of this parable unmistakably clear in verse 35: "So also my heavenly Father will do to every one of you, if you do not forgive your brother from your heart."

So let's start there.

(1) *When we refuse to forgive, we set ourselves up to be turned over to "tormentors."*

There is a sense in which Jesus was referring to ultimate, eternal torment—those who remain intransigent in their unforgiveness give no credible evidence that they have ever been forgiven themselves; if that is the case, they will be subject to the eternal wrath and judgment of God.

But there's another application of Jesus' words: people who refuse to forgive those who sin against them may be turned over to more immediate, temporal "jailers" or "tormentors."

What are some of those tormentors? I believe that many of the chronic mental, emotional, and physical disorders people struggle with today are rooted in bitterness and unforgiveness. Not all, of course. But a growing body of research is beginning to confirm that anger and resentment are responsible for many of our physiological problems.

Newsweek reported that this particular line of study is one of the hottest fields of research in clinical psychology today. Emotions such as bitterness, rage, and hostility are being linked with blood pressure increases, hormonal changes, impaired immune function, and memory loss. "Every time you feel unforgiveness," said the executive director of one research group, "you are more likely to develop a health problem."[2]

According to an article in *Reader's Digest*, "Dr. John Sarno, a professor of rehabilitation medicine at NYU School of Medicine believes that almost all back pain is somehow rooted in bottled-up emotions."[3] His observations over thirty years of work with patients have convinced him that repressed rage and anxiety eventually manifest themselves as muscle spasms, nerve dysfunction, and other forms of pain and numbness.

It's amazing how our countenances reveal the telltale signs of bitterness.

Another *Newsweek* feature outlined a study that confirmed that people who score high on tests for anger, hostility, or depression have higher blood levels of a certain type of protein strongly linked to heart risk—as much as twice as high![4]

Interestingly, in fact, both the words *anger* and *angina* share the same Greek root.

Please hear me. I'm not suggesting for a moment that every physical ache or pain is caused by bitterness or unforgiveness. But in many cases, I am convinced it's true. You see, God never intended our bodies to hold up under the weight of unresolved conflict and bitterness.

It even shows in our faces—it's amazing how our countenances reveal the telltale signs of bitterness and unforgiveness. You can just look at some people today and see the lines etched by years of harbored hurt turned to bitterness.

I don't want to make anyone who suffers from organically rooted diseases feel the least bit condemned, or to suggest that you shouldn't pursue medical treatment for physical ailments. Please understand that.

But Jesus linked a refusal to forgive with God turning us over to tormentors. If I were dealing with persistent, unexplainable symptoms, I'd at least *ask* the Lord if there's anything He's trying to get my attention about, any unforgiveness or bitterness that might be causing unnecessary physical, emotional, or mental issues.

I know of one woman who did just that. She turned in a prayer card at the beginning of a conference where I was speaking, requesting prayer for a back problem. At the close of the conference she sent a note saying:

After I made the decision to forgive my sister and mother, I
noticed that the pain in my back was gone. I have had this pain
for several months (*tormentors?*). I believe I have been healed
in my heart and in my body by stepping out to forgive.

I want to be clear—being a forgiving person will not guar-
antee you a pain-free life. But I can't help but wonder how much
pain we might be spared and how much money we could save on
doctors' and therapists' bills if we refused to let any bitterness
take root in our hearts.

Feeling Unforgiven

Here's another conclusion we can draw from this passage:

(2) *When we refuse to forgive, we cannot experience God's love
and forgiveness.*

Read again Jesus' words at the end of the parable in Matthew
18 about the unforgiving servant: "So also my heavenly Father
will do to every one of you, if you do not forgive your brother
from your heart" (v. 35).

Most of us have quoted many times this petition from the
Lord's Prayer: "Forgive us our debts as we forgive our
debtors." The wording of that request should lead us to ask ourselves, "What if God only forgave me to the extent that I've
been willing to forgive those who've sinned against *me?*" It's
sobering to think about.

And it's something we can't ignore, for in the verses that

follow directly after the Lord's Prayer in Matthew 6, we hear Jesus saying, "If you forgive others their trespasses, your heavenly Father will also forgive you, but if you do not forgive others their trespasses, neither will your Father forgive your trespasses" (vv. 14–15).

Strong words. They challenge us to examine our hearts to see if we have ever truly been forgiven. As John Piper has said, "If we hold fast to an unforgiving spirit, we will not be forgiven by God. If we continue on in that way, then we will not go to heaven, because heaven is the dwelling place of forgiven people."[5] The point is not that a forgiving spirit causes us to merit God's forgiveness, but simply that forgiven people forgive others, and that those who persistently refuse to forgive others have no basis to claim to have been forgiven by God.

When we refuse to forgive, something is blocked in our relationship with the Father.

But even forgiven people sometimes struggle to forgive. And unforgiveness always affects our relationship with God.

I have met many believers who find it difficult to accept and experience God's love and forgiveness. There can be any number of different reasons for that. But I believe that one of the biggest is their refusal to forgive others. These words of Jesus on the subject of unforgiveness are so stark and direct, we who are saved by grace yet unforgiving in our hearts find ourselves looking for loopholes, dodging the obvious, trying to convince ourselves that He must have meant something less exacting. Certainly He who knows how deep our hurt goes couldn't possibly expect full forgiveness from us! *Could He?*

Yet in reality, we find nowhere to hide. "Blessed are the merciful," He said, "for they shall receive mercy" (Matthew 5:7) —implying, we can assume, that those of us who are *not* merciful toward others shouldn't expect to find ourselves on the receiving end of that promise.

When we refuse to forgive, something is blocked in our relationship with the Father. The Scripture affirms what our own experience confirms—a clear connection between our willingness to extend forgiveness to others, and our ability to appropriate and experience His forgiveness for our sins.

Those who hold on to bitterness, who refuse to forgive, cannot hope to enjoy the full, sweet taste of His compassion and mercy.

Satan's Footsteps

There's one more important observation about unforgiveness that I want to make: (3) *When we refuse to forgive others, we give Satan an advantage in our lives*—both individually and in our corporate fellowship.

In trying to show the Corinthians what was causing the disunity in their fellowship, the apostle Paul talked to them about the importance of forgiveness. There was apparently someone among them whose sin had been exposed, someone who had "caused pain" to their fellowship (2 Corinthians 2:5) but had presumably repented and sought restoration. Yet instead of this being cause for great joy, forgiveness toward him from some was coming slowly, reluctantly, being held back in reserve, making it even harder for him to enter into the grace of his Father's mercy and begin living in freedom.

So Paul urged the Corinthians to "forgive and comfort" their repentant brother (v. 7), as Paul himself had done, "for your sakes in the presence of Christ, *so that no advantage would be taken of us by Satan,* for we are not ignorant of his schemes" (vv. 10–11 NASB).

The Devil always wins when we fail to forgive.

When we refuse to forgive, he is given an opportunity to take advantage of us—to win arguments in our minds, to have his way in our relationships, and to desensitize our hearts to the Spirit's voice.

That's why the Scripture exhorts us: "Be angry and do not sin; do not let the sun go down on your anger, and give no opportunity to the devil" (Ephesians 4:26–27). We may at times have righteous anger against sin. But if we let that anger turn to bitterness or fester in our hearts, we provide a beachhead for Satan's activity in our lives.

I saw this progression vividly illustrated in the life of a young woman I know. When "Corinne" (not her real name) was a little girl, she began to nurse hurt feelings toward various individuals, including church members who unfairly attacked her pastor father and a well-meaning mother who was somewhat overbearing and at times harsh and too quick with her correction.

Corinne allowed the hurt to turn to anger, which fueled inner resentment and boiled into intense bitterness and turmoil. Ultimately, all that bitterness came to the surface and spilled over, with disastrous consequences for this young woman, as well as for her family and friends. Satan had a field day in her life and this "good girl from a good Christian home" found herself plunged into depths of spiritual darkness that would once have been unthinkable.

When we shut the door on forgiveness, we open it for Satan to have an inroad into our life, giving him just the weapon he needs to get an advantage over us.

Dare to Be Disciplined

Yet even with these grim reminders, we still often find ourselves choosing the path of unforgiveness. And if we choose it long enough, we become something we neither intended nor wanted. We become bitter people—whether we're willing to admit it or not.

As is the case with any sin, the more we practice it, the more it becomes ingrained as a normal pattern of behavior. The more we hold on to our hurts, anger, and bitterness, the more we become slaves to unforgiveness (see Romans 6:16). And the longer we stay in that condition, the more difficult it becomes for those chains to be broken.

Bitterness grows in us when we fail to see the trouble and pain in our lives from God's point of view, and when our *expectations* of what life should be diverge from the *reality* of what life really is.

The fact is, life in a sinful, fallen world is not easy. As the apostle Paul reminds us:

The whole creation groans and labors with birth pangs . . . even we ourselves groan within ourselves, eagerly waiting for the adoption, the redemption of our body. (Romans 8:22–23 NKJV)

Hebrews 12 is a rich chapter that gives us perspective on the hardships we face as believers. It reminds us that God uses the experiences of our lives—even the difficult ones—perhaps *especially* the difficult ones—to do something special in us: to discipline us "for our good" (v. 10).

Yes, *for our good!*

This is not a natural way of thinking—about as natural as a child looking forward to being disciplined or corrected by his parents! As this passage declares, and we have all experienced,

For the moment all discipline seems painful rather than pleasant, but
later it yields the peaceful fruit of righteousness to those who have been
trained by it. (v. 11)

God is not implying that what has occurred in our lives is no
big deal. If you have been wounded or mistreated in some way,
He is not telling you to just to shake it off, get a grip, grow up,
and get on with it.

No, the teaching of Hebrews 12 should encourage us that
God considers these matters weighty enough to require His special care and attention. He wants to use these painful experiences
for our spiritual training and maturity. They are part of His eternal purpose and His plan to mold and shape us into the image of
Jesus, so He can be glorified through our lives.

That perspective offers us hope—it encourages us and gives
us stamina to persevere, knowing there is an end and a worth-
while goal in sight. It enables us to endure the pain and to embrace whatever process God knows is needed for our training
and growth. And it is the pathway to spiritual wholeness, healing, and well-being. That's exactly what the writer to the Hebrews goes on to say:

Therefore lift your drooping hands and strengthen your weak knees,
and make straight paths for your feet, so that what is lame may not be
put out of joint but rather be healed. (vv. 12–13)

God has a purpose in this. You can trust Him. In fact, His

willingness to become involved in your life—even as the disciplining Father—gives evidence not of His disapproval but of His love. When received with a tender, submissive heart, God's chastening reassures us that we are in relationship with Him, that we belong to Him.

Instead of resenting the people He uses as instruments in our discipline or responding sinfully to the problems we face, we are challenged to:

Strive for peace with everyone, and for the holiness without which no one will see the Lord. (v. 14)

The author then reminds us of God's provision for dealing with life's painful circumstances, as well as what will happen if we don't receive and appropriate that provision:

See to it that no one fails to obtain the grace of God; that no "root of bitterness" springs up and causes trouble, and by it many become defiled. (v. 15)

I am convinced that sexual sin is almost invariably linked to a root of bitterness, as are many other sins and issues.

When we get hurt, no matter how serious the offense or how deep the wound, God has grace available to help us deal with the offense and forgive the offender. At that point, we have one of two choices: We can acknowledge our need and humbly reach out to Him for His grace to forgive and release the offender. Or we can resist Him, fail to receive His grace, and hold on to the hurt.

If we take the latter course, bitterness will take root in the soil of our hearts. In time, that root will spring up and cause trouble for us and for others around us who will be affected by our unforgiving spirit.

Verse 16 expands on this concept by illustrating one way that bitterness commonly manifests itself in people's lives: "That no one is *sexually immoral* or unholy like Esau, who sold his birthright for a single meal."

At the risk of oversimplifying, after years of dealing with people who have "fallen" into various types of immorality, I am convinced that sexual sin is almost invariably linked to a root of bitterness, as are many other sins and issues.

A girl's spirit is wounded by her abusive or absentee father—instead of looking to God for grace, she resents her dad and looks for love in bed with her boyfriend. A young man is molested by an adult male or doesn't receive appropriate male affection from his dad. Failing to receive the grace God offers, he becomes bitter and turns to illicit relationships with other men to try to satisfy the unmet needs in his heart. A man feels disrespected by his wife (or a woman, neglected by her husband). Instead of turning to God for grace, he (or she) becomes vulnerable to the advances of a colleague at work or some other sexual sin.

They sell their spiritual birthright for—what? Bondage, perversion, shame, generations of broken lives and homes. I've seen it over and over again.

Once that root of bitterness is allowed to spring up, their lives—and who knows how many other lives—become troubled and defiled.

That's exactly what happened to one man I know who, along with his wife, had served the Lord and enjoyed a fruitful ministry for many years. Over a period of time, however, "Dan" allowed seeds of spiritual pride and self-deception to subtly take root in his heart. As he said recently, recalling those days, "What I didn't know was that I was setting myself up for bitterness and hurt."

Sure enough, when some ministry opportunities did not materialize as he had hoped they would, Dan became disappointed with God.

In failing to appropriate God's grace to deal with the disappointment, he opened the door for bitterness to creep in—first toward the Lord, then in his relationship with his wife. Over a period of time, he closed his heart toward both the Lord and his wife, at which point the Enemy, seizing the opportunity, began to bombard him with temptations toward lust.

Having already chosen to resist God's grace, he was a sitting target. When the temptation became more intense and he succumbed, he blamed God and became even more bitter. "People didn't seem to understand me as they used to, and God didn't seem to respond as He once had," he said. "The problem was, in my pride and self-deception, I had become deeply bitter, opening wide the door to all kinds of defilement."

It was only a matter of time before that root of bitterness grew up into full-fledged adultery. "The next thing I knew, I was throwing away everything I knew to be good and right." Wrong became right, evil became good, black became white for this man.

Now that he is finally broken, repentant, and in the process of restoration after a long, hard sojourn in "the far country," Dan looks back and says, "I'm overwhelmed at what my spiritual *pride* and *bitterness* caused me to do."

A similar progression can be seen in the life of Corinne, the young woman I referred to earlier in this chapter. Rather than receiving God's grace to deal with childhood hurts through forgiveness, she allowed a root of bitterness to spring up in her life. In so doing, she gave Satan an advantage—a foothold, just the opportunity he wanted.

During her childhood and later when she was a student in a Bible college, she became tormented by demonic voices and appearances and was drawn into various types of occult and sexual practices too unspeakable to print. In the process, she nearly ended up taking her own life and left a swath of damage in the lives of those affected in the wake of her self-destructive behavior.

Corinne now recognizes that her failure to forgive caused her to forfeit the grace God wanted to give her to deal with the pain she suffered as a child, and that in so doing, she gave much ground in her life over to the Enemy.

Only by God's grace and the earnest rescue efforts of grace-filled believers is this young woman recovering and beginning to find freedom through forgiveness.

A Reason for Not Refusing

A "root of bitterness"—it may not seem like a big deal. In fact, given the circumstances, it may seem perfectly under-standable and justifiable. But be assured it is no small mat-ter. Unacknowledged and un-addressed, its poison will affect and infect you and others beyond anything you ever imagined possible.

When you are unjustly maligned or injured by the ac-tions of others—perhaps a member of your extended family, or your employer, or someone you go to church with—bitterness may feel like a birthright. It can become

Grace is there, because He *is there.*

your safety zone. You may feel incapable of any other response. But it is a fallback position doomed to failure.

Not only is it sin; it is senseless.

The cure for bitterness is to trust both His hand and His heart and to "draw near with confidence to the throne of grace, so that [you] may receive mercy and find grace to help in time of need" (Hebrews 4:16 NASB). Yes, grace is there, because *He* is there.

Through this circumstance—no matter how painful or difficult—you have both the potential and the opportunity to be made more like Christ. This is the Father's highest purpose in your life, that you become "conformed to the image of his Son" (Romans 8:29). Even Jesus Himself, by the Father's divine plan and purpose, was perfected "through suffering" (Hebrews 2:10), not only to gain our eternal salvation but also to know what it feels like to be treated harshly, to be taken advantage of, to be misunderstood—as you have been.

The root of bitterness will infest every inch of ground in your life if you let it. But God invites you—*urges* you—to reach out and receive His grace. In so doing, your heart will be set free from the vise of unforgiveness; you will be released to love and serve Him and others. No longer will that root of bitterness trouble you and "defile" others; instead, His grace will flow through you to others, blessing everything you touch.

Making It Personal

✸ As you read this chapter, particularly the statements on p. 58, did the Lord put His finger on any root of bitterness or un- forgiveness in your heart? If so, how has that bitterness mani- fested itself (e.g., the sins listed in Ephesians 4:31)?

✸ Can you identify any chronic stresses or pressures in your life (e.g., physical, emotional, mental, relational, financial) that could possibly be traced back to a bitter, unforgiving spirit? Ask the Lord to show you if there is a connection.

✸ Can you identify any ways that a root of bitterness (past or present) has resulted in one or more of these consequences in your life:

  • affected your ability to experience God's love and forgiveness

  • given Satan a foothold in your life

  • "defiled" others around you

✸ What is one area of your life in which you need to receive God's grace so that a root of bitterness does not spring up in your heart? Will you cry out to Him for grace in that area?

FORGIVENESS OUGHT TO BE LIKE A CANCELLED
NOTE—TORN IN TWO AND BURNED UP,
SO THAT IT CAN NEVER BE SHOWN AGAINST ONE.

—*HENRY WARD BEECHER*

CHAPTER THREE

THE PROMISE
OF FORGIVENESS

I know just enough about computers, as they say, to be dangerous. But one thing I've learned the hard way is the meaning of that little button that's spelled D-E-L.

That's right. The delete key. (I'm guessing you know about that one yourself.)

Like you, I can think of times when I was working away at something on my computer and accidentally pressed the delete button, only to watch all my hard work vanish into thin air, leaving behind nothing but a blank screen of forgotten words.

Yes, I know the software programmers thought ahead about people like me, making sure a little prompt would flash up and ask me if I was really, *really sure* I wanted to throw out a half-day's work in one fell swoop. But I've been known to brush aside their kind warnings and move right on, losing everything I had done. It's easy to do.

I wish the delete key was so easy to press in real life.

In many ways, what happens when we trash a computer document is a vivid picture of what takes place when we truly forgive someone for an offense they've thrust upon us. We eliminate it. We clear the record. We treat it as if the sin never occurred in the first place. Isn't that the way God has forgiven us?

And isn't that how He tells us to forgive others—"forgiving each other as the Lord has forgiven you" (Colossians 3:13)?

As believers, we are told that God has forgiven "all our trespasses, by canceling the record of debt that stood against us with its legal demands. This he set aside, nailing it to the cross" (Colossians 2:13–14).

At one time, the "record" was right there, accusing us, exposing us, vindicating His righteous anger against us. But with one press of the delete key, our holy, merciful God erased the whole thing. Nothing was saved on a backup disk. Nothing printed out in hard copy. Nothing stored in a separate folder or filing cabinet in case it proved useful to whip it out again someday.

All of it, deleted. Forever. All because of Christ's death on the cross—in our place. Debt canceled.

This was God's way of dealing with what we had done to Him. And that is what He asks us to do with others' sins against us.

I believe most of us, in our dealings with others and the pain they've brought into our lives, would love to get to that point. We'd love to see the pain and bitterness gone, a nonissue, done away with.

But the problem is, we know that just pushing a button won't make all the feelings disappear. It won't totally undo the damage or put everything back like it was. So why even try? Why set ourselves up for disappointment, perhaps leaving the door open for this to happen again and to hurt us even worse? Why go to all the emotional trouble of transacting forgiveness if it won't repair the gaping hole in our hearts, at least not for a good long time?

Why would God ask for such a thing?

Because of a promise.

Behind His Back

Yes, as much as anything we could say about forgiveness, this truth seems to capture it well: *forgiveness is a promise*—a promise never to bring up that sin against that person again— not to God, not to the person who committed it, not to anyone else. It is a deliberate decision to deal with another's sin by doing away with it, pressing the delete button, wiping it off our slate. With the promise of forgiveness, we relinquish our "right" to punish the offender or to make him pay—his record has been cleared.

Sometimes a woman will come up to me and say, "I've forgiven my husband" or "I've forgiven so-and-so"—and then she'll begin listing all the hurtful things that person has done to her. While I can applaud her for recognizing what she needs to do, her own words reveal that she hasn't truly, fully forgiven—because forgiveness is a promise.

It's a promise God has made to us. "As far as the east is from the west, so far has he removed our transgressions from us" (Psalm 103:12 NIV). Yes, what we did to Him was real. What we *continue* to do against Him is real. But by the atoning blood of His Son, God has chosen not to remember our offenses. He has put them behind His back.

That's a promise we can take all the way to eternity.

This matter of forgiveness is truly at the core—the very heart—of the gospel. Even our excuses for *not* forgiving keep bringing us back to the cross, back to where forgiveness was perfectly applied, not to a group of people who'd gone through all the right steps to become forgivable, but to us—to people who didn't deserve it, didn't know we needed it—perhaps didn't even want it!

We of all people should appreciate the joy of forgiveness . . . by knowing what a treasure it is to be purely and perfectly forgiven.

But beyond that, when we extend to others the forgiveness that Christ extended to us on the cross, we reflect the mercy and grace of God to a world that desperately needs to be forgiven.

"Can You Forgive the Germans?"

Ernest ("Ernie") Cassutto was a Dutch Jew, who after nearly two and a half years of running and hiding, had finally been captured by the Nazis, another sad casualty of the madness that had swept through World War II Europe. His fiancée Hetty, who, like Ernie, had come to faith in Christ, had also been rounded up and caught, her final destination the gas chambers of Auschwitz.

In his moving book *The Last Jew of Rotterdam,*[1] Ernie tells of kneeling on the floor of his prison cell one unending day, reading the Bible. He came across the passage where the three young friends of Daniel, Shadrach, Meshach, and Abednego, had been cast into the fiery furnace where the Lord Himself had met them. Suddenly, he said, "The 'fourth man' was also with me. No one, not even the Nazis could shut Him out. Jesus met with me in my prison cell, and He had something to ask me:

"'Can you forgive the Germans, Ernie? Can you pray for them and love them?'"

Ernie's shoulders stiffened. "Forgive them? Love them? O Jesus, how can I? They've taken me prisoner. They've killed Hetty. Forgive them? It's too much for me, Lord."

But in the aching silence that echoed off the walls of his prison block, snatches of memories began to flash through his mind. He could see the page in Hetty's journal where she had written the words of Matthew 5:44—"Love your enemies and pray for those who persecute you." He thought of Jesus, shamed and tortured and bloodied by human hate, the same Jesus who forgave His murderers from the cross, the same Jesus who even now was asking him to forgive another unthinkable offense.

"I can't, Lord." What else can a man really say? How impossible is forgiveness of that magnitude! "But if You will help me, I will try. Please. Help me."

And one by one, the chains of hatred, anger, and bitterness began to snap in Ernie's heart. He could look up. He could almost feel in his body a new freedom of movement, the relief of having been shorn of the weight of his burden. For though he was still in prison, Ernie was free.

As he recounted it years later, "One more Hebrew child was being delivered out of a fiery furnace."

One day after the war, after his release, Ernie received a phone call from the wife of the commandant who had overseen the prison where Ernie had been held. The man was now sick and dying of a contagious disease, and his wife wanted Ernie to come visit him.

Yes? No?

We can only imagine the distance that resided between these two responses, and how hard his heart had to be leaning toward refusing. He had already forgiven; he had relinquished his hatred. That should have been enough. To look into those evil eyes again, much less to run the risk of being infected with the same contagion and facing death once again—yes?

As he wrestled with his dilemma, Ernie's father urged him, "Jesus tells us we must forgive our enemies. Go see him."

He went.

And there he was—his once cruel captor—now weak and struggling to breathe. Ernie tried to speak, but words failed. At that point, "a voice from inside me urged . . . 'Go kiss him.'"

"I could not believe what I had heard. Kiss him?"

But the voice would not keep quiet. "Kiss him. I will protect you."

"Timidly," Ernie recalled, "I leaned forward and kissed his forehead. He burst into tears. And as he wept, he apologized over and over for the wrong he had done.

"Then I knew that he didn't just need *my* forgiveness; he needed God's mercy. I told him about Jesus, how the Jewish Messiah died to atone for the sins of the world."

And right then and there, Ernest Cassutto led his former jailer to Jesus.

Walking away, Ernie thought again of those words from Matthew 5:44. "The Lord had taught me another lesson on how to love my enemy . . . and this time, he had also taught my enemy to love me."

You know as well as I do, an experience like that cannot be faked or manufactured. For a Holocaust survivor, for you and for me, forgiveness is indeed a supernatural undertaking. It's not something we can do ourselves. As Corrie ten Boom—a woman who dealt with the same challenges during the same exact timeframe—wrote in *The Hiding Place*, "It is not on our forgiveness, any more than on our own goodness, that the world's healing hinges, but on His."

So while forgiveness is indeed costly, it is not beyond the means of those who have Christ's life flowing within them. When God tells us to love our enemies, He also gives us the love to go along with the command.

Yes, you can do this . . . because *He* can do this.

That's a promise.

Not Me, Not This

Do you have a situation where forgiveness seems impossible? Perhaps you're thinking, "I just can't forgive this person for what he's done to me. It's too painful to deal with. He's done it too many times. He's hurt me too deeply."

I wouldn't begin to deny the "deeply hurt" part. If you were to tell me your story or share it with a close friend, we would see it in your eyes. We would hear it in your voice. We would know that this sin has injured you in a deep and tender place.

But you must ask yourself—we must all ask ourselves—"Is my ability or willingness to forgive based on the magnitude of the offense?" In other words, is there a threshold of pain beyond which we are not required to forgive, one perhaps where it is *impossible* to forgive?

The Scripture reminds us that God has "cast *all* our sins into the depths of the sea" (Micah 7:19). Not some, but all.

These sins include things like the scorning mockery and insults of those who "despised" Him (Psalm 22:6–7), who totally "rejected" everything about His character, His person, His reason for living (Isaiah 53:3). It's one thing to be disliked; it's quite another to be *despised*—hated, spit upon, ridiculed, humiliated, betrayed, and wanted dead. Add to these the sins of our own, the ones we know so well, those that contributed to the guilt Jesus bore on the cross.

Yet this is the same God "who blots out your transgression" and who "remembers your sins no more" (Isaiah 43:25 NIV), who found us "dead in our trespasses" and made us "alive together with Christ" because of His "great love" for us (Ephesians 2:4–5).

You may not feel any natural "great love" toward the one who brought such shipwreck into your life—the one who trampled on your marriage vows, or the one who abused you as a child, or the one who cheated you out of thousands of dollars.

No one would expect you to.

But the power—and

When it comes to forgiveness, our Lord would not command us to do something that He would not enable us to do.

the beauty—of the transformed Christian life is that "it is God who works in you both *to will* and *to do* for His good pleasure" (Philippians 2:13 NKJV).

It will never be the depth of *your* love that causes you to forgive such heartless acts and attitudes. It will never be within *your* power to overlook the wicked lies and wild justifications of those who have made you distrustful of just about everybody. It will be —it can *only* be—the love of Christ transplanted into your believing heart that can exchange your weakness for His strength.

And so because He has forgiven us—and because of His boundless life which now indwells us—*what offense is too great for us to forgive?*

"To be a Christian," C. S. Lewis said, "means to forgive the inexcusable, because God has forgiven the inexcusable in us." When it comes to forgiveness, our Lord would not command us to do something that He would not enable us to do. Or that He hasn't done Himself.

Making Them Pay

Another thing we may find ourselves thinking as we grapple with unforgiveness is this: "If I forgive them, that means they're off the hook!"

We sometimes feel that, if we forgive someone, justice will not be served. They'll get off scot-free. We'll be doing little more than giving them permission to do wrong again, seeing how easily we let them get away with it this time.

From a human perspective, this makes sense. But our minds need to be renewed to think God's way. According to God's Word, wrongdoers will get their just due. But *we're* not the ones responsible to mete out the penalty:

Beloved, never avenge yourselves, but leave it to the wrath of God, for it is written, "Vengeance is mine, I will repay," says the Lord. (Romans 12:19)

When we try to keep someone "on the hook," we're assuming a role that belongs to God alone. It's our way of keeping the prison keys in our own hands, of wanting to be in charge of how justice is administered.

It's that old, rotten business of debt collecting.

Read those words from Romans 12 again: "Never avenge yourselves . . . leave it to the wrath of God . . . 'Vengeance is mine, I will repay,' says the Lord." What Paul is saying is this: letting the offender off *your* hook doesn't mean he's off *God's* hook. Forgiveness releases the accused from your custody and turns him over to God—the righteous Judge—the one and only One who is both able and responsible for meting out justice.

And so what feels like the height of unfairness, what seems to be nothing more than giving our offender the pass, actually becomes for us a step of freedom.

Joseph's story in the last part of Genesis is one of the most moving biblical illustrations of this truth. Repeatedly wronged throughout his life—misjudged, treated unfairly, and falsely accused as both a boy and a man—Joseph came to a place in his life where he could have wreaked his full vengeance on the ones who started it all—his brothers. He had the right, the authority, and all the means at his disposal to bring them to justice. In fact, they were trembling at his feet, fully expecting it. The show was over.

But listen to Joseph's response to his distraught brothers: "Don't be afraid. *Am I in the place of God?*" (Genesis 50:19 NIV).

What wise, humble words! *Am I in the place of God? Is it my job to make you pay for what you've done? Do I really want the added burden of this after all I've been through already? Isn't it foolish to think that revenge could be as sweet as advertised—sweet enough to make up for the pain of all these years?*

I want to clarify a couple of important points here: when the Bible teaches us to forgive those who sin against us—to let them off our "hook"—it does not minimize the seriousness of their sin or suggest that what they have done is *okay*. Nor does it suggest that we should knowingly enable the person to keep sinning or relieve them of the consequences for their wrongdoing.

Take, for example, abusive situations, criminal activities, unethical things you may know concerning people at work. It is not wrong (and may be necessary) to report someone, to turn guilty offenders over to the appropriate authorities who can hold them accountable, to be part of helping them face the reality of what they've done.

But if your heart in doing so is bitter or vengeful—if you are being vindictive, obsessed with revenge, inwardly hoping to see their downfall—then you are still holding on to the controls. Even if you manage to bring the offender to justice, you won't experience the freedom God offers. In reality, you are keeping yourself imprisoned by your offender.

It's true that sometimes we have to deal with fools in our lives. I'm reminded, for example, of the story of Abigail and Nabal in the Old Testament—a man whose name actually meant "fool." David (not yet King David) had sent messengers to Nabal, asking for nothing more than reasonable remuneration for his protection of Nabal's flocks and herds. But Nabal had run David's men off his property, hurling insults behind them to hasten their departure.

Upon hearing this report, David was angered. He ordered his men to strap on their swords and go seek their revenge. When Abigail realized what was happening, she rushed out in hot pursuit to defend her foolish husband, to work for his best interests even though he likely deserved everything David was planning to dish out.

When you read the whole account in 1 Samuel 25, you see that Abigail didn't cover or make excuses for her husband in talking to David. She didn't defend his foolish behavior. Nor did she try to tear him down or just get someone to take her side. She didn't deny what kind of man Nabal was, but acted in his best interests—seeking the kind of blessing and protection he would have sought for himself if he had been under control and in his right mind.

Please hear me—I am not suggesting that we should shield

others at all costs from the consequences of their actions, or just take anything they inflict on us and sit there doing nothing.[2]

I am saying that their judgment before God is not ours to accelerate. God will deal with the Nabals in our lives. In fact, He dealt with *this* one. When Abigail returned to her drunken husband and told him what she had done, the shock caused his heart to fail. Within ten days, he was dead.

But this wise and discerning woman could go on living without regret, knowing she was not the one who had brought about her husband's destruction. Living with a fool had not forced her to act like one herself.

Proverbs 11:21 says, "Be assured, an evil person will not go unpunished, but the offspring of the righteous will be delivered." We must seek God's wisdom (and perhaps seek counsel from a pastor or another mature believer) in dealing day-to-day with the Nabals in our lives. But we must remember that their real business is with God. He will repay.

God's Love—and Lorna's

Several years ago, I met a dear woman named Lorna Wilkinson, whose husband—not unlike Nabal—had brought a great deal of discord and mistrust into their marriage. He was an alcoholic; his condition had worsened over the years, bringing with it all the turmoil that tends to accompany substance abuse: financial pressure, irresponsibility, the chaos of never being able to depend on him, never knowing if he'd be where he said he would.

This had gone on for twenty-one long years, always with the hope that things would get better, that he would change. Finally, Lorna decided that she had been through enough. She came to the conclusion that divorce was the only way out, the best way she knew to salvage what remained of her life.

So she took the step. She filed all the paperwork, asked him to leave, and prepared to move on.

She was not yet a believer. But providentially, right at that critical juncture in her life, she "happened" to tune in to a *Revive Our Hearts* radio program, when I was teaching about forgiveness. Her heart was gripped as she learned of the incredible forgiveness God offers through Christ, the way He deals with our sin by perfectly releasing us, thus enabling us to extend the same kind of forgiveness to others.

Day after day, this needy woman continued to listen to the broadcast, her thirsty heart drinking in the truth of the Word. Within a short period of time, her eyes had been opened and she was brought to faith in Christ.

But her divorce was still moving forward . . . until the day her phone rang. It was her husband, saying he was sick.

"At the time, I was still frustrated and angry to some degree," she admits. "I said, 'Why are you calling me? Why don't you call 911?'"

He did. Just in time. Her husband was having a heart attack.

Extended family began to gather at the hospital, not sure if he was going to make it. To hear Lorna tell it, part of her wanted to be there too—although part of her wanted to be done with him. But somewhere in the depths of her heart, the Lord seemed to be saying, "Go whisper in your husband's ear that he doesn't have to worry about a place to live. Tell him he can come home."

That day, amid a tangle of tubes and wires and other life-saving devices, Lorna gave her husband the most revitalizing gift of all: the gift of forgiveness.

By God's grace, he did recover. He came home. He was a changed man. Miraculously, he no longer had the urge to smoke or drink. He landed a full-time job and began working faithfully to provide for his family. Newfound love entered their home, a desire to pray and worship, a focus on lasting priorities. There were flowers, postcards, candlelit dinners. Everything.

Early in the process of restoration, there were moments when those old feelings would flood back in Lorna's heart. "Lord, I can't do this," she would cry out in prayer. "I cannot love him the way You intended me to love. But I am asking You, Lord, to give me *Your* love, to just let it flow through me to this man."

And God's love slowly began to melt the awful memories. One by one, she began entering into each of those descriptive phrases in 1 Corinthians 13—"Love is patient and kind . . . does not insist on its own way . . . rejoices with the truth . . . bears all things, believes all things, hopes all things, endures all things."

As God's love began to fill their home, Lorna and her husband started to experience the kind of marriage she had always dreamed of but had given up hope of ever having. In fact, four months after they were reconciled, Lorna's husband woke her early one morning to say, "I now know that a man should love his wife the way God has loved us. I want to tell you, Lorna, at this moment, I love you that way."

These were the last words she would ever hear from his lips. Within hours, a second massive heart attack would take him home to be with the Lord.

Imagine where Lorna and her children might be today if she had chosen the logical way, the natural way, the vengeful way—the bitter path of unforgiveness. Imagine the lives that would still be in shambles, the regrets that would have lingered for a lifetime.

A few years after her husband's death, I sat in a studio, listening with tears streaming down my face, as Lorna shared her story in a radio interview.

"Do not give up on your marriage," she urged the listeners. "Do not give up on your spouse. Take it to the Lord in prayer and always remember—what you are not able to do for yourself, He will do it for you and in you."

Even when you can't see the results of forgiveness, you can still know you've done what God requires of you.

The Delete Key

I can't begin to tell you how many people have written or responded to me, telling me that by God's grace they have chosen, like Lorna, to press the delete key—to forgive, to clear the record.

Has this automatically fixed everything for those individuals? No. Has it changed their circumstances at all? Not always. Not immediately.

Certainly, not every marriage is remedied the way Lorna's was, even by forgiveness. But even when you can't see the results—though the situation may not clear up entirely or get any better at all—you can still know that you've done what God has required of you. You can *continue* to forgive as His grace and love flow through you. And you can walk in peace—His peace.

As Paul wrote in Philippians 4:7 (NKJV), the peace of God will "guard" your *heart*—your feelings, your emotions. It will "guard" your *mind*—your thoughts, your decisions. That's because His peace does its hard work in your life "through Christ Jesus," who knows what it means—and what it costs—to forgive it all.

That's the promise of God to you.

Making It Personal

✷ Is there a "Nabal" in your life that you need to entrust to
God? How can you respond in a way that demonstrates forgiveness, courage, wisdom, and faith?

✷ What fears, feelings, or reservations may have kept you from
forgiving someone who has sinned against you? How does
God's Word address those concerns?

✷ *"Forgiveness is a promise—a promise never to bring up that sin
against that person again, not to God, not to the person who committed it, not to anyone else."* Based on that description, is
there anyone you still need to forgive? Will you press the
delete button and let it go?

I SAY TO THE GLORY OF GOD AND IN UTTER HUMILITY
THAT WHENEVER I SEE MYSELF BEFORE GOD
AND REALIZE EVEN SOMETHING OF
WHAT MY BLESSED LORD HAS DONE FOR ME,
I AM READY TO FORGIVE ANYBODY ANYTHING.

—*D. MARTYN LLOYD-JONES*

CHAPTER FOUR

FORGIVING FOR JESUS' SAKE

For many years, I was a part of a team that conducts revival meetings in local churches across the United States.[1] I remember one particular church where the Spirit of God moved in an unusual way, bringing many church members to brokenness and repentance. During the course of those weeks, a doctor fell under intense conviction and finally confessed to his wife his most devastating, well-kept secret: he had been carrying on an adulterous relationship with a nurse in his office.

Maybe you've been where this wife found herself. Maybe you *are* there. And the shock, betrayal, disgrace, and selfishness of it all still make your insides hurt.

I suppose none of us can ever quite know how we'd react initially to that kind of revelation. This man's wife didn't know either. Of course, the shock was huge and the pain gut-wrenching. But somehow, as she struggled to process the revelation of her husband's infidelity, she found herself inexplicably overwhelmed with the awareness that she *must* forgive him. It wasn't that she was living in some dream world of self-denial, but as she later recounted, "How could I *not* forgive him, when God had forgiven me so completely?"

Incredibly, carried by the grace of God, she even sat down later and wrote a note to the "other woman," assuring her that she had been forgiven. The very next day, the woman showed up at her door and exclaimed through her tears, "Because of your forgiveness, I have come to know the Lord."

How can that happen in real life? With real people with real feelings?

Maybe the better question is not "how?" but "why?"

The answer is not some sort of superficial, sentimental response we're supposed to be able to muster up toward those who have hurt us. It's not blithely shrugging off the offense as if nothing had happened.

In his classic devotional book *My Utmost for His Highest*, Oswald Chambers reminds us that at the crux of the whole issue of forgiveness is the cross of Christ. There is no forgiveness possible apart from the cross—and the cross is no trifling matter.

> It is shallow nonsense to say that God forgives us because He is love. . . . The love of God means Calvary—nothing less; the love of God is spelt on the Cross, and nowhere else. The only ground on which God can forgive me is the Cross of my Lord.[2]

We tend to forget that. We somehow have the idea that God has forgiven us purely out of His kindness, just because He wanted to. Forgiveness is what we sort of expect from a God who wouldn't mind going out of His way to be extra nice to us.

But it makes a huge difference when we realize the ground on which our forgiveness was procured. If we are to forgive others as God has forgiven us, we need to understand how He forgave us.

Calvary required an agony we cannot fully comprehend. On the cross, Jesus took our sin upon Himself, enduring the wrenching consequence of broken fellowship with the Father—the One He adored, the One from whom He had never experienced a moment's separation. That is impossible for us to fully grasp.

We can at best only imagine what the Father and Son must have endured when, for the first time ever, the cost of our sin interrupted their eternal fellowship.

But it is from this "tremendous tragedy," Chambers writes,

that our forgiveness is won. "To put forgiveness on any other ground is unconscious blasphemy."[3]

Those are strong words. So are these: "In him we have redemption *through his blood*, the forgiveness of our trespasses. . . . For he himself is our peace, who has made us both one and has broken down *in his flesh* the dividing wall of hostility" (Ephesians 1:7; 2:14).

Forgiveness isn't meant to be free and easy. It is hard. It is costly. It is painful.

But this is the only way it can be real—real like God's forgiveness of us is real—real enough to truly change us.

How Can This Be?

If you're a child of God, the ordeal you're undergoing will be used to take you deeper into His heart.

You've probably heard it said that nothing can come into the life of a believer without first coming across God's desk, without first being filtered through His eternal love and will for us. We see this so clearly, of course, in the story of Job, where God allowed Satan to inflict a defined measure of pain in Job's life.

This means, then, that whatever crisis you've faced, whatever has happened in your life to cause unforgiveness to well up in your heart, God could have stopped it. But He didn't.

I'll admit that this is one of the more difficult teachings of Scripture. We cannot fathom the complexities of how a holy, sovereign God interfaces with a sinful world to fulfill His eternal purposes. But one of the verses we know so well and repeat so often reveals the hope that dwells within this truth—enough hope to give us good reason for persevering beyond our point of understanding: "We know that for those who love God all things work together for good, for those who are the called according to his purpose" (Romans 8:28).

But how can this be true? How can we be sure? How can something so evil ever be redeemed or result in anything of value?

At least in part, the answer lies in the fact that those "whom he foreknew, he also predestined to be *conformed to the image of his Son*" (v. 29).

If you're a child of God, the ordeal you're undergoing, however wrong or unfair or heartless it may be or may have been, in His providence and skillful hands will be used to take you somewhere good—deeper into His heart, to a place of greater dependence and trust, more perfectly refined into the likeness of Christ.

Think again of the cross and its implications for those who suffer (as we all must to some degree) the vile consequences of life in a fallen world. Here is undoubtedly the most heinous wrong ever committed in the universe, where, in the prayerful

words of the early believers, wicked men were "gathered together against your holy servant Jesus . . . to do whatever your
hand and your plan had predestined to take place" (Acts
4:27–28).

Who would ever have planned Calvary? Who could have
seen one good thing coming from such an atrocity?

Only the God who could see ahead to resurrection.

And He is the same One who has measured the scope of
your pain and injustice, who closely monitors the depth and
length and height of every trial that every one of His children
endures, and who will not allow into your life a single circumstance that will thwart or derail His eternal, loving plan for your
life.

If even the scourge of the cross could not stop Him from
completing the plan He had for His Son, how could any past or
current difficulty in your life—as bad as it may be—*even begin*
to surpass His desire or His ability to complete the plan He has
for you?

He will use even this, dear one, to accomplish His redemptive, sanctifying work in and through your life.

Three Sides of Forgiveness

Perhaps the offense that has affected your life the hardest,
the one that comes most quickly to mind when you think about
the need to forgive, is a wound from the distant past—a childhood experience or a teenage encounter.

Or perhaps it's something that's ongoing, a back-and-forth battle between you and your mate, or one of your grown children, or a relative, or a roommate, or a co-worker. Perhaps it's gotten so bad and has progressed for so long that your relationship with this person is practically severed. Just the thought of that person stirs up anger and heartache and all manner of negative emotions within you.

You avoid him. You do your best to ignore her. The last thing you want to do is to pick up the phone and call. You just try not to think about it.

The apostle Paul, in the shortest of his biblical letters, introduces us to a situation with both past and ongoing implications —where harm had been done, trust had been broken, and one man's action had caused a problem that wasn't going away.

It's the real-life story of Philemon, a man of apparent wealth and influence who had come to Christ at some point under Paul's ministry. Over time, the fruit of Philemon's Christian faith had become evident in his life. Paul commended him as a man full of love, one who had opened his home as a meeting place for the church in his hometown of Colossae. By all accounts, Philemon was a devout man of God.

But one of his slaves, Onesimus, had run away—not only with his skill and labor but also, it seems, with an undisclosed amount of stolen property. Fleeing to Rome, some 1,200 miles away, Onesimus had probably hoped to lose himself in the crowd, joining the thousands of other runaways who had taken the same risk.

In God's all-wise providence, however, Onesimus had come into contact with Paul, who was currently in Rome under house arrest while awaiting trial. As they talked, the gospel left its mark. The one-time slave surrendered himself to Jesus Christ. And he became—rather than a shiftless fugitive—a friend and assistant to the great apostle Paul.

Paul knew, however, that Onesimus couldn't avoid forever the responsibility for what he had done to Philemon. He must go back, ask forgiveness, and pursue reconciliation. In order to help him avoid being picked up by slave catchers, not to mention being misunderstood upon his arrival in Colossae, Paul sent along a companion to protect him . . . as well as a letter to explain things.

Thanks to that letter, we get to watch this story unfold.

The three main characters in this account provide insight into three "factors" in the forgiveness equation. At various points in life, we are likely to find ourselves in one or the other of these roles.

First, we see Onesimus, the offender, now going back to make right the wrongs of the past and seek reconciliation. Then there is Paul, the peacemaker, working to bring two parties together and restore their fellowship. (Thank God for the peacemakers!)

In the third position, we find Philemon—the one who had been wronged, the one who was being asked to forgive—not only to forgive but to restore a continuing relationship with this one who had caused him such harm and distress. To do so, he had to be willing to absorb the wrong that had been done to him, to swallow the losses he had incurred. Furthermore, he had to be willing to look at his runaway slave in a whole new light—as a brother in Christ.

We're not told how this situation played out. But perhaps— and this is speculating a little—history gives us a faint hint as to what happened.

A few decades later, one of the early church fathers wrote a letter to the church in Ephesus, in which he referred to the pastor who served there as "Onesimus, a man of inexpressible love." Granted, there's no way to be certain that this is the same Onesimus as the one in the story of Philemon. But it's possible.

We do know this—any offender who is restored by God's grace is not simply returned to where he was before it all took place. Through the Lord's great mercy, guilty sinners can be declared guilt-free and restored to lives of greater fruitfulness than they ever dreamed possible.

Isn't that what happened to us at the cross?

And shouldn't that be our great hope, as we extend forgiveness toward others, that they would enjoy the freedom of living with a changed identity, just as we have—we who have been declared "a new creation" through the forgiveness of Christ? Paul summed it up succinctly: "All this is from God, who through Christ reconciled us to himself and *gave us* the ministry of reconciliation" (2 Corinthians 5:18).

Paul knew the wonder of that redeeming, transforming grace as well as anyone. Once a great blasphemer and persecutor of Christ and His church, he had been forgiven a debt infinitely beyond his ability ever to repay. More than that, he had become a joint-heir with Christ, an undeserving recipient of all the riches of God in Christ Jesus.

The rest of the apostle's earthly life was poured out in helping others experience and extend this amazing grace that reconciles men to God and to one another—people like Onesimus, like Philemon, like you and me.

That's what the cross is all about.

Forgiving Yourself?

Yes, it should stir us to our very core to see just how outrageously costly the forgiveness of our sins was to God. Our redemption hurt Him more deeply than any human has ever suffered. It drew blood. It required Calvary.

But it required even more than that. It required an act only God could perform. To quote from Chambers again, "Forgiveness is the divine miracle of grace."[4] It is something only God can do.

So if it seems impossible for you to forgive this person who has hurt you so deeply—and who perhaps continues to treat you harshly and unfairly—guess what? It *is* impossible—for you! But nothing is too difficult for God. And He is the One who can do the forgiving, the reconciling, through you.

Yes, only God can forgive sins. Remember the time in Jesus' early ministry (Luke 5:17–26) when the men brought their para-

lyzed friend to be healed, letting him down through the roof because the crowd was pressing so hard around Him? Jesus said to
the paralyzed man, "Your sins are forgiven you," to which the
Pharisees protested, "Who is this who speaks blasphemies? Who
can forgive sins but God alone?"

There was a whole lot wrong with their attitude, to be sure,
but not with their question. *Who can forgive sins but God alone?*
No one.

This is important to remember especially when your issue
isn't an unresolved conflict with someone else but is something
you've done yourself—when all the regret, all the shame, all the
guilt leads you to say, as I've often heard expressed, "I just can't
forgive myself."

Perhaps you're having a hard time getting past a "grass-is-
greener" decision you made that cost you a good job and a lot of
your long-term security. It could be a moment of negligence
where you failed to keep one of your children safe from danger.
It could be an abortion you had ten years ago. It could be any of
a million things.

A well-meaning friend or counselor may tell you that forgiving yourself is your first step toward healing and recovery.
The problem is, nowhere in the Scripture do we find God in-
structing us to deal with our heartaches this way. Rather, He
urges us to receive *His* forgiveness.

In fact, Paul writes, "If God is for us, who can be against us?
He who did not spare his own Son but gave him up for us all,
how will he not also with him graciously give us all things? Who

shall bring any charge against God's elect? *It is God who justifies*" (Romans 8:31–33).

If we feel compelled to forgive ourselves, mustn't it be an indication that we either doubt God's forgiveness of us or that we're simply unwilling to receive it? If God's forgiveness is not good enough for us, then what's so special about ours? What makes our forgiveness able to do what His cannot? If He has forgiven us, our slate is clean. What more is there to forgive?

Forgiveness is too big a miracle to expect of ourselves. To rely on it is to wish for something that can never be.

God is your forgiver—your one and only forgiver. When Jesus gave His life on the cross to pay for your sin, He said, "It is finished!" The price has been paid in full. Through faith in His finished work, you are forgiven. Nothing you have done—nothing you could ever do—can absolve you of an iota of your guilt.

Forgiveness isn't something you can give yourself. It is something He has purchased for you.

William Cowper (1731–1800) was a gifted and prolific British writer and poet, a contemporary and close friend of John

Newton. Throughout his lifetime, Cowper struggled with recurring bouts of severe depression and mental and emotional instability.

At one point, in a fit of anxiety and near madness, he attempted to take his own life—first intending to throw himself in a river, then to ingest a lethal dose of opium, then by falling on a knife, and finally, unable to succeed through other means, by hanging himself. The strap with which he hanged himself broke and he fell unconscious to the floor before being rescued.

An article published some years subsequent to his death described the excruciating remorse and anguish Cowper experienced in retrospect:

> He felt for himself a contempt not to be expressed or imagined . . . ; he felt as if he had offended God so deeply that his guilt could never be forgiven, and his whole heart was filled with tumultuous pangs of despair.[5]

After recovering physically from the ordeal, however, Cowper came to realize that no sin can create a stain too great for God to erase. Out of the torturous experience, he was moved to pen those words that have pointed millions of guilt-ridden sinners to the cross—the only source of true relief and release:

> There is a fountain filled with blood drawn from Emmanuel's veins;

And sinners plunged beneath that flood lose all their guilty
stains.

The dying thief rejoiced to see that fountain in his day;
And there may I, though vile as he, wash all my sins away.

Fully forgiven. Is that your experience?

Christ's sacrifice at Calvary is sufficient to forgive every
sin, even yours. Forgiveness isn't something you can give yourself. It is something He has purchased for you. Receive it by
faith and be free.

Seeds of the Gospel

Thinking that we need to forgive ourselves is one example
of how we sometimes try to add to the gospel. The apostle Paul
was quite stern and direct with those in his day who wouldn't accept the good news as complete and fully adequate, those who
insisted on tagging on their own conditions and requirements.
We have been forgiven in Christ, and that is enough.

But if trying to forgive ourselves is an attempt to add to the
gospel, unforgiveness of others is a sure way to detract from it.
Think of it this way. We are forgiven sinners, having received
the grace of God. And so we go out into our world telling lost
sinners that they need what we have. "He can forgive you; He
can cleanse you; He can set you free," we confidently assert.

But these people know us. They work next to us at the

office. They cut our hair. They sit with us at lunch. They live on our street. And they hear us. They hear the way we talk about that ex-mate, that in-law, that man who messed up our kitchen flooring, that teacher who didn't give our child a big enough role in the school play.

And so our message about the gospel of Christ rings a little hollow. It's hard for God's grace and mercy to be all that believable when we—the very ones who claim to be forgiven by Him —refuse to forgive others.

On the other hand, there is no more credible evidence to the world that the gospel we proclaim is real than when we extend His forgiveness to others.

Ask the dozens of recent converts in the Santhal tribe in rural eastern Nepal. When a woman who was a member of the tribe chose to follow Christ, her family and neighbors beat her so badly that she had to be hospitalized and finally died from the wounds. Local police arrested and charged several people with her murder. However, Christians living in the village responded by expressing their forgiveness of the murderers and asking to have the charges dropped.

Amazed by such a display of grace, the villagers' hearts were softened, hundreds flocked to hear the gospel, many have turned to Christ, and a new church has been started in the village.[6]

Ask the apostle Paul. Ask him to remember a day when he was standing just to the side of an angry mob, watching over the coats of those who were killing one of those "blasphemers" named Stephen.

Ask him about some powerful words Stephen cried out

above the noise of an afternoon stoning spectacle. I'm sure that as Paul later became more aware of who Christ really was, as he learned of the things Jesus had said while dying on the cross, he thought back to these similar words of Stephen:

"Lord, do not hold this sin against them" (Acts 7:60).

Here was a man—Stephen—who had put both pieces together. What he had received *from* Christ, he extended to his murderers *through* Christ. The cross had made the connection. Forgiveness in. Forgiveness out.

A Silent Sword

If you've seen the classic movie *Ben-Hur*, you remember how, as a young man, Judah Ben-Hur is wrongly accused of assaulting a Roman centurion. As a result, his family's home and possessions are confiscated. His mother and sister are imprisoned in an underground cell, where through a combination of hunger and vermin they both contract leprosy. Judah himself is lashed as a galley slave in the belly of a Roman warship.

And the one responsible for it all is his childhood friend, Messala, who turned him in to the Romans.

Through the passing years, Judah becomes consumed with hatred and bitterness toward the Romans in general and Messala in particular—obsessed with a burning desire for revenge. When circumstances converge allowing him to return to his homeland, his heart roars afresh with anger, as he is reminded of the disastrous losses inflicted on his family.

Reunited with his childhood sweetheart, Esther, the weight of his pain presses against him even harder. While talking with her, he spews the full venom of his fury, the rage that is forever tormenting him.

As it happens, that very day, Esther has been out listening to a man named Jesus. "If you had heard this man from Nazareth . . . ," she says wistfully, recalling His words. "He said, 'Blessed are the merciful, for they shall obtain mercy. Blessed are the peacemakers, for they shall be called the children of God.' The voice I heard on the hill today said, '*Love* your enemy. *Do good* to those that despitefully use you.'"

Judah is unmoved and reacts angrily to such a notion. He has no interest in mercy and peacemaking, no intention of loving his enemies.

Then Esther responds tearfully: "It was Judah Ben-Hur I loved! What has become of him? *You seem to be now the very thing you set out to destroy, giving evil for evil. Hatred is turning you to stone.*" And then the words that stung most deeply—

"*It's as though you had become Messala.*"

Stop and let that sink in for a moment. Is it possible that you are becoming just like the one who has hurt you? Have you become a different person, someone you never intended to be, displaying attitudes and characteristics you detest in others? Is hatred hardening your heart and turning it to stone?

God wants to set you free. And that release will take place for you at the very same place that it did in the fictional life of Judah Ben-Hur.

As the story unfolds, Judah ends up in Jerusalem on the very day Jesus is being led away to be crucified. He follows the procession to Golgotha until he finds himself standing directly underneath the shadow of that center cross, watching the blood flow down Jesus' tortured body onto the ground below.

As he gazes upon the Savior, the love of Christ finally penetrates Judah's hardened heart. Silently, without saying a word, he believes and receives that love. His face is visibly transformed, as the years of bitterness and hatred are washed away by the love and the blood and the grace of Jesus.

In the closing scene of the movie, Judah recounts that life-changing moment to Esther: "I heard Him say, *'Father, forgive them,* for they know not what they do' . . . and I felt His voice take the sword out of my hand."

Let me ask you a question. Is there still a sword in your hand? A sword of bitterness, resentment, vengeance, unforgiveness? If so, I want to invite you to take a trip to Calvary. Stand beneath the cross of Jesus and see what He endured to purchase your forgiveness, the agony He went through so you could be free. Hear Him extend pardon to His persecutors. And let His voice take the sword out of your hand.

Will you become—like the Lord Jesus—broken bread and poured out wine, a reflection of God's matchless grace, a living demonstration of the beauty and the power of forgiveness?

Forgiveness in. Forgiveness out. That's the way of the cross, the heart of the gospel.

Making It Personal

- Is there some sin in your past for which you still struggle to "feel forgiven"? What is the role of (a) the cross and (b) faith in making it possible for us to fully experience the reality of God's forgiveness?
- How well does your life reflect the forgiving heart of God toward sinners? Do you make the gospel believable to others by the way you respond to those who wrong you?
- Take some time to meditate on the cross. What does the death of Christ mean for you—as a sinner? As one who has been sinned against?

THE GLORY OF CHRISTIANITY IS
TO CONQUER BY FORGIVENESS.

—*WILLIAM BLAKE*

CHAPTER FIVE

THE ART OF FORGIVENESS

But how?

We've spent the first half of this book considering some of the major whys of forgiveness. But like everything else in the Christian life, forgiving others is much more than what-fors and how-comes. Ours is an active faith. It is made alive and appealing only when our nouns turn into verbs.

On the other side of "choosing forgiveness" is the

kind of life God intended for you when He sent His Son to die for your sin—the freedom to bless others, to walk unhindered by bitterness and resentment, to relate confidently with God and with the people around you, and most important to be a living, walking display of the gospel and grace of Christ.

But how do you get there? How do you come to the place where forgiveness can do its healing work, both in you and in your offender?

How do you become like the woman who wrote to share, "I have chosen to forgive my husband for the sexual relationship he had with his girlfriend before we met. I've been holding on to this hurt for four years. I'm excited now to embrace him and tell him he has been released."

Our faith is made alive and appealing only when our nouns turn into verbs.

How do you find freedom from an issue that's been seething and simmering for a good part of your lifetime, like the person who told me, "The Lord had me release a prisoner that I've held captive for over sixteen years. Now God can restore the years that the locusts have eaten."

How do you overcome an offense so entangled in your heart that it's shaped the person you are and the way you react to all of life, like the woman who said, "I was molested by my brothers and father for as long as I could remember until I was sixteen. This led to years of letting men abuse my body. I never knew how to have a healthy relationship with men. I have held this hatred for so long in my heart. But I am choosing to release it and give it to God."

I've seen the Lord give people grace to forgive in situations that are almost beyond belief.

"Last February," one woman wrote, "a neighbor broke into our home and killed my husband, kidnapped me, raped me, and then killed himself. I was left with three small children." She went on to say how she took "great satisfaction in hoping that he [her attacker] was burning in hell," and how "the only way I could deal with the situation was to know he was being punished."

God began to deal with her heart at a women's conference where I spoke on forgiveness. She knew the pain was killing her. She knew she needed to forgive. And once she did, she was able to experience God's peace and rid herself of needing to know what ultimately happened to her assailant. "Now I am free. I don't know if he is in hell or heaven. But I know God is in control, and I can praise Him."

I've watched the Lord reconcile and restore relationships between people who could hardly stand to be in the same room together. I remember being approached at the close of another conference by two such women who wanted to tell me their story. They were mother and daughter-in-law. The young woman, every bit of nine months pregnant, had been married to the other woman's son for four years.

But through all the years they had known each other, they had never gotten along. In fact, their dislike for each other had grown pretty intense. I don't know that they could have even explained anymore what their complaint with each other was all about, but they had certainly gotten to the place where everything about the other one bothered them.

I'm sure you know how that can happen. Maybe it's happened to you.

Though this mother-in-law was on the host committee for the conference, she had not invited her daughter-in-law to attend—"I knew she wouldn't come if I invited her."

But she did come. Uninvited.

Wouldn't you know it, God found them there, sitting in different sections of the auditorium. And during the course of that afternoon, as I shared about the importance of forgiveness, one of them made the first move. I don't even know which one, but all I do know is that they both ended up in the prayer room, in each other's arms, seeking and finding one another's forgiveness.

I'm telling you, it can happen—in any situation—in *your* situation—as God gives the grace and as you make the choice to do what He's calling you to do.

But how?

Who Did It?

I want to suggest three practical steps you can take—both to accelerate and cement your forgiveness of others. I don't mean to suggest that forgiveness is easy or to reduce it to a three-step formula. I realize that painful memories, emotions, and relationships may all be involved and may require further healing.

But I have found these steps helpful for jump-starting that process and setting people on the journey to freedom.

As a starting place in the pathway of forgiveness, (1) *identify the people who have wronged you and the ways(s) they have sinned against you.*

Here's a simple way to do that: take a blank sheet of paper and draw two lines from top to bottom, forming three even columns down the page. (See next page for example.) In the left column, write the names of all those who have sinned against you, anyone with whom you still have unresolved issues of the heart.

You know who they

> *Forgiveness does not mean pretending that the offense never happened.*

Name	What they've done	How I've responded

are. Mother, father, stepparent, brother, sister, former employer, former pastor, neighbor, son or daughter, ex-mate—make the list.

Then in the middle column—next to the names you've just listed—write out the specific offense (or offenses) each one has committed against you. How did they wrong you? Be specific.

"Wait," you may wonder, "what's the point of bringing all this stuff back up again? I thought we were supposed to 'forgive and forget,' to bury these things. Now you're telling me to list it all!"

It's important to realize that forgiveness does not mean pretending that the offense never happened. That's not honest. That's denial. True forgiveness is not about mind games and dream worlds—it's not about escaping from reality. It's about *facing* reality and dealing with it God's way.

These things that others did to you were wrong. They have hurt you. And God does not want you to run *away* from your pain but to run *to Him* in the *midst* of your pain—to fly head-on into the full fury of it, to face it, to let Him meet you right where it hurts and give you the grace to be set free from any bondage to that hurt.

But one important disclaimer here: in encouraging you to list the ways others have sinned against you, I am *not* suggesting that you should try dredging up things from your past that you have no memory of, as some would counsel. God is able—and sometimes chooses—to erase painful memories from our minds. There is no value—in fact, I think much harm can be done—in conjuring up memories that God may have mercifully removed.

If there's someone you need to forgive, you probably won't need to go hunting to know who it is and why. Deal with the issues you know need to be dealt with, the ones that are clear in your mind, and trust the Lord to bring to mind any other offenses you may need to forgive.

Write down any inflicted wounds from the past or present that you are consciously aware of. Don't hide from these. See them for the genuine sins they are.

Clear about This?

Now, some would perhaps stop right here. They would think that the mere process of naming those who have wounded you would be healing enough. They might even suggest that you burn this list in the fireplace, symbolically letting all the pain and suffering go up in smoke.

But I believe the Bible leads us to do something else, something deeper, something more healing and holy—(2) *Make sure your conscience is clear toward each of the individuals on your list.*

That's what the third column on your paper is for. Ask yourself, "How have I responded to this person?" Then record your answer.

- ❋ Have you blessed them?
- ❋ Have you loved them?
- ❋ Have you prayed for them?
- ❋ Have you forgiven them?

Or would it be more honest to say that you have withheld love from them, resented them, and been angry with them?

Have you bad-mouthed your ex-mate to your children? Have you put up walls toward that neighbor who's constantly in your business or that co-worker who ridicules you for your beliefs? Have you given negative reports about that person who painted you in a bad light to your friends? Have you subtly retaliated against the in-law or the sibling who has made your life difficult by giving them the silent treatment—disengaging from the relationship, rather than pressing through to love them?

You can't really forgive until your conscience is clear toward those who have sinned against you, until you've let God fashion His love in your heart toward those who have failed you.

The truth is that you're not responsible for what goes in that middle column (assuming their offense wasn't in response to your sin against them!). You didn't ask for it, didn't invite it, don't deserve it. But you *are* responsible—solely and fully responsible —for what goes in the third column.

And if your response has not been Christlike, then you need to go back to that person and seek his or her forgiveness for the way you've sinned against them.*

Again, this line of thinking sometimes draws a knee-jerk (and quite understandable) reaction: "Wait a minute! This person sinned against *me*! And now you're saying I've got to go ask *him* to forgive *me* for what I did to him?!"

Yes.

Perhaps, of course, you've honestly done nothing wrong in your heart toward this person. You haven't wanted revenge. You haven't talked about her behind her back. You haven't rolled your eyes at him when he says he's sorry.

I hope that's the case. But it's usually not.

More often than not, the *offended* becomes an *offender* in his response to the offense. In the mind of the one who has been offended, that response may be completely justified: *He deserves it. . . . It's his fault, not mine. . . .*

Regardless of what may have provoked our response, if we have sinned against a spouse, a parent, a friend, an old acquaintance,

---

* Clearly, there are some situations where it would not be appropriate go back and establish contact with an offender. If you are unsure, I would encourage you to seek godly counsel from your pastor or another mature believer.

an authority figure—whomever—we need to ask their forgiveness just as if we were the one who started this whole thing
in the first place. We need to take responsibility for our sinful
response.

"Well," you acknowledge, "I may have been responsible for
5 percent of what happened to break up our marriage. But *95 percent or more* of it was his fault!"

Okay. Then assume 100 percent responsibility for your "5
percent" and ask forgiveness.

You may find, of course, as you allow God to search your
heart that the percentages are really not quite as skewed as
you've been leading yourself to believe. Granted, there are situations where we can be totally innocent of all guilt, where we did
little or absolutely nothing at all to bring this about, situations
where we've continued to forgive and move on without holding
a grudge.

But for the most part, we're quick to overlook our share of
blame—just as quick as the other person is. That usually leaves a
lot of unclaimed responsibility lying around, where it can keep
on spreading its poison, perpetuating the damage.

In the Sermon on the Mount, Jesus reminds us that it's a lot
easier to see the failures in others' lives than it is to see our own
needs. We tend to look at everyone else's sins with a micro-
scope, while looking at our own with a telescope!

Jesus emphasizes the importance of dealing with our own
sins before we try to deal with others' failures.

Why do you see the speck that is in your brother's eye, but do not notice

the log that is in your own eye? Or how can you say to your brother,

"Let me take the speck out of your eye," when there is the log in your

own eye? You hypocrite, first take the log out of your own eye, and

then you will see clearly to take the speck out of your brother's eye.

(Matthew 7:3–5)

This isn't to minimize what your "brother" may have done. It's just that it's hard to be objective about *his* sin, or effective at helping him get rid of it, if *you* haven't confessed your sin. Not to speak of being hypocritical!

So be honest: Has someone else's sin begotten sin in your own life? Then confess it. To them, if it's possible and appropriate. Not in a way that excuses you, not in a way that blames them for pushing you to it, not in a way that leads you into even more sin by stirring up your anger against them.

God is saying, "You take responsibility for your part." Have you?

If not, humble yourself. Go and seek forgiveness. Be sure your conscience is clear.

Your Choice

Once you've identified those people who have wronged you, once your conscience is clear with the Lord and with those individuals—you've sought forgiveness for anything you've done to them, either in contributing to what happened or in reacting to them with sinful attitudes and behaviors—it's time to take the next—and what may be the hardest—step in your journey.

(3) *Choose to fully forgive every person who has sinned against you.*

This is where the proverbial rubber meets the road. This is where all the tender and wounded parts of your emotions may cry out in self-protection and protest. And this is where the Enemy will work hard to keep you from going all the way with God and doing what you know you need to do.

But this is where you have to go if you want to be free.

Choose to forgive each individual (or group) who has sinned against you. Clear their record. Press the delete button. Release them from your custody.

You don't have to feel like it. You don't have to want to. But if you want to be an obedient child of God, you've got to forgive.

Chances are, when you started this book, when God put it on your heart—again—to deal with this issue that's been so front and center in your life for so many years, you knew we were going to get here eventually. There's just no detour around this point in the journey to freedom in Christ.

"If you hold anything against anyone, forgive him" (Mark 11:25 NIV).

"But what if they haven't asked for forgiveness? What if they don't think they did anything wrong?"

Well, sadly, their unwillingness to repent will keep them from receiving God's forgiveness (the forgiveness that matters most) and from having a right relationship with Him. And it will limit their capacity to have a fully restored relationship with you and others.

But though that person's hardness will affect his well-being and his relationships until he faces and deals with his sin, though it may keep him in bondage, no one can force *you* to be bound as a prisoner in your own heart—not as long as you take the bold step to forgive. That is a choice you can and must make, regardless of where the other person is in their journey.

As you respond to the Lord in this matter, be sure not to stop short of actually forgiving your offenders. I've heard sincere, well-meaning people pray, "Lord, please *help me to forgive* this person." I've heard others say, "I know I need to forgive him . . ." I don't doubt their sincerity, *but that's not enough.* Don't just ask God for help; don't just talk about your need to forgive. Go all the way. Say, "Lord, by Your grace and in obedience to You, I *choose* to forgive—to clear their record, to press the delete button, to release the offender, to let the offense go. I *do* forgive!"

Forgive Terrorists?

Gracia Burnham and her husband, Martin, made that choice under circumstances that most would have considered unforgivable.

Abducted by a Philippine terrorist group while on a brief break from their missionary responsibilities, this couple endured more than a year of torture, want, and abuse, being pushed and shoved in pointless circles through the tangles of a tropical jungle. In June 2002, when the national military attempted a rescue of the hostages, Gracia escaped, wounded but freed. Martin was killed in the firefight.

After their whole long ordeal together, Gracia had to walk out of the jungle alone.

In her poignant telling of their story in her book *In the Presence of My Enemies,* as well as her follow-up book *To Fly Again,* she takes us back through some of the brutal realities of hostage life, nightmarish scenes it's hard to imagine anyone surviving.

The maddening confinement of being chained to a tree for hours, sleeping straight up, forced to beg for daily needs.

The pain of being wracked with incessant diarrhea, heightened by the indignity of having no place to retreat in private, no means of cleaning herself, and no escape from the unsanitary conditions that only worsened the disease.

The exhaustion of being strapped down with fifty-pound loads

> *"Anger in the face of trauma is understandable. But that doesn't make it productive."*
>
> —*Gracia Burnham*

of gear to walk miles over rugged ground, with precious little on the outside to shield away the elements and even less in their stomachs to sustain their weak, weary bodies.

Torture.

And when not mortally afraid—anger.

"As Martin and I squatted around the cooking fire waiting for our portion," she recalls, "we would carefully watch the server pile rice on other plates but then give us only two-thirds of a cupful, solely because we were non-Filipino and non-Muslim. I wanted to scream."[1]

Yet even in the screeching, relentless jungle, even with heavily armed captors laughing and poking fun—men who had no right to be so callously, so coldheartedly standing between Gracia and home, between Gracia and her children, between Gracia and a warm bath or a home-cooked meal—even in these extreme conditions, God was working in Gracia's heart.

She writes, "I found that as long as I blamed the Abu Sayyaf [the group holding them hostage], my heart remained in turmoil. I blamed the terrorists; I blamed the Philippine military for their ineptness; I blamed the American government for not waving some magic wand to free us; I even blamed God because . . . well, He's in control of everything, isn't He?"

But gradually her perspective began to change: "I began to realize that my resentment wasn't serving any useful purpose. . . . Anger in the face of trauma is understandable. But that doesn't make it productive. . . . The alternative, of course, was to forgive, even without the benefit of an apology from the offender.

I could *choose* to forgive, all by myself."

And as she forgave, God did again what He does so well. Her anger cooled down. The hurt began easing away.

"But then a new day would dawn," she admits, "and a new injustice would erupt. I would be faced with a fresh need to forgive. This was a conscious decision I would have to make and remake as time went by. In fact, it became a pattern. And therein lay a path back to self-control and composure.

"I did not pray, 'God, help me forgive,'" she recalls. "To do so would have been to dodge my own responsibility. . . . The task was squarely mine, although *once I chose to obey, God certainly gave me the strength to do so* (emphasis added)."[2]

Gracia is safely back home now in a small Kansas town, raising her three children, living a life that's more in line with what we can relate to and understand. Her battles today aren't the rigors of hostage survival but the everyday trauma of a kid who keeps forgetting to take the trash out to the curb, a friend who makes a derogatory wisecrack, some family member who says something unkind.

But she would tell you: the same forgiveness model applies.

We identify the sin. We clear our conscience toward the offender. We choose—yes, Lord, we choose—to forgive.

For Better and the Worst

Do you still think you just can't do it? Do you think your situation is just too hard?

Several years ago, I watched a dear friend go through deep waters in this whole matter of forgiveness—not just once, but again and again and again. I vividly recall the day her husband of twenty-three years confessed to her that he had been involved in a sexual affair with another woman for six months.

That part—the sheer fact that he had broken their wedding vows—was bad enough. But to add salt to the wound, he wasn't sure if he was ready to give it up or what he was going to do about it.

Things went on pretty much that same way for more than a year. "He would tell me the affair was over," she wrote recently as she rehearsed the story, "but all along he still had it going. He actually showed no evidence of true brokenness and grief over his sin, and continued in it, sometimes almost flaunting it in my face. This hurt me and our children more than I could ever describe."

But somehow, God gave this brokenhearted wife the grace to cling to the Lord, to forgive her wayward husband, and to keep loving him faithfully, even in the midst of her intense pain and with his apparent lack of sorrow over his sin.

"I didn't *feel* forgiving at first," she said. "My initial reaction was extreme anger, then great hurt. But I remember that first night after finding out about the affair, I fell on my face before God with an open Bible and poured out my heart to Him.

"I did not understand why God would allow this to happen to me, but I did know that it had to pass through His loving hands to get to me and that He wanted to use it for good in some way and for His ultimate glory.

"*I chose to forgive my husband that night,* even though he had not asked me for it, and though I was trembling all over and almost numb with pain. I could only think of Christ on the cross and how He asked His Father to forgive those who were killing Him."

So was that the end of it? Once she chose to forgive, did their home become a happy place again, where everyone interacted freely and looked forward to game night on Fridays?

No. "Over those next thirteen months, there were many more times when I would be devastated by something my husband did or said in relation to the affair, yet God continued to enable me to show him forgiveness, even when he was still living in sin.

"I could never 'work up' forgiveness like that. I am weak and sinful, and I realized during those tough times that God was pouring His grace out on me to give me the ability to forgive."

In the midst of this painful process, as my friend chose the pathway of forgiveness, she experienced the presence and power of God in an extraordinary way:

Something amazing happened in my life as I continued to forgive my husband. God gave me such freedom and joy in the midst of the pain I was experiencing. Somehow God let me see the whole experience, not as something to despise, but as *a gift to embrace.*

There's no way, humanly speaking, to explain it. God truly allowed me to rejoice in my suffering and to see it as an opportunity to suffer in a very small way as He had when He was rejected.

These are not the words of a Bible teacher dealing with theory. This is not someone detached enough to be satisfied with pat answers. This is the testimony of a woman who has been there, who knows what it feels like, what it costs, what it means . . . a woman whose faith has been tried in the furnace of affliction and has come forth as gold.

In time, God mercifully brought her husband to genuine repentance and graciously restored his broken life and their marriage —something I am convinced never would have happened apart from the willingness of this wounded wife to forgive (and keep on forgiving)—long before she could see the outcome or had any assurance that his heart would ever be changed.

Here's how she concluded her written testimony:

When we choose to forgive others, even when they are not broken themselves, God pours out freedom, grace, peace, joy, love—and even forgiveness itself into our hearts. It takes your breath away when you experience it yourself. *It takes you to depths with God that you never could have reached except through this mysterious path.*

Wow.

Do you realize what that means? Whatever you are going through, however great or small the wrong that has been done to you, the choice to forgive could mean your most precious days with the Lord are right in front of you.

Yes, forgiveness is supernatural. Yes, it's something only God can do. Yes, it is far beyond our flesh-and-blood ability. But if you are a child of God, you have been infused with the same power that He "worked in Christ when he raised him from the dead" (Ephesians 1:20)—think of that! That means you have His limitless power within you—supernatural ability to extend forgiveness for "unforgivable" offenses. By His enabling power, you can forgive others with the very grace and forgiveness that you have received from God for *your* sins.

So choose it! Do it! Don't wait to feel like it or to figure out how it will all work out. Ultimately, forgiveness is not an emotion. It is an act of your will—an act of faith. Don't harbor that bitterness for even one more day.

Your issue may be a monumental one like some of those you've read about in this book—or worse. Or it may be something that seems insignificant by comparison—so minor that you may have convinced yourself it's not such a big deal—that it's okay to continue on with this simmering resentment.

Whether the offense is so large that you think you *can't* forgive, or so small that you think you don't *have* to forgive, either way, you'll stay in prison until you release it into the cleansing stream of God's fathomless mercy, and *let . . . it . . . go!*

This is His will for you in Christ Jesus. And you can choose to take hold of it!

If you've still not taken that plunge into the ocean of His forgiveness, cry out to Him right now: "Oh, God, for Jesus' sake— as You have forgiven me, I choose to forgive him. I choose to forgive her. I choose to forgive each person who has sinned against me."

"I choose to forgive!"

Making It Personal

✿ "Now that you know these things, you will be blessed if you
do them" (John 13:17 NIV).

WHATEVER MEN EXPECT,
THEY SOON COME TO THINK THEY HAVE A RIGHT TO;
THE SENSE OF DISAPPOINTMENT CAN,
WITH VERY LITTLE SKILL ON OUR PART,
BE TURNED INTO A SENSE OF INJURY.

—*SCREWTAPE TO WORMWOOD*
THE SCREWTAPE LETTERS, C.S. LEWIS

ANGRY
AT GOD

In the matter of Drusky versus God—God has won."

That's how the Associated Press report, dated March 15, 1999, started out.

It went on to explain: "A Pennsylvania man's lawsuit naming God as a defendant has been thrown out by a court in Syracuse [NY]." After a longtime battle with his former employer (then called U.S. Steel), Donald Drusky had blamed God—officially—for failing to bring him justice as a result of his firing by the company some thirty years earlier.

"Defendant God is the sovereign ruler of the universe," the lawsuit read, "and took no corrective action against the leaders of his church and his nation for their extremely serious wrongs which ruined the life of Donald S. Drusky."

According to the news report, "U.S. district Judge Norman Mordue threw out the case. Mordue ruled that the suit—which also named former U.S. presidents Ronald Reagan and George Bush, the major U.S. television networks, all 50 states, every single American, all federal judges, and the 100th through 105th congresses as defendants—was frivolous."

As ludicrous as all this sounds to rational people, in a sense Drusky's diatribe is different only in degree from what I hear a lot of people saying these days.

As I read the letters and e-mails people send to our ministry and listen to people share their stories, one of the recurring themes is: "I'm angry."

"Angry at my husband."

"Angry at my children."

"Angry at my parents."

"Angry at my pastor."

And sometimes, after they get through all those layers, I hear them express something that is really at the heart of the matter:

"I'm angry at God."

Even godly people like Gracia Burnham are sometimes

tempted to direct their resentment toward God. You may have picked up on it in the last chapter. In listing the many causes of her plight while being trapped as a hostage in the Philippines, she singled out the people. She named names. She saw faces. Then she pointed to a face she couldn't see, yet someone she felt must somehow be at least partially responsible for her suffering—

God.

It came out in the excerpt I shared from her testimony: "I even blamed God," she said, "because . . . well, He's in control of everything, isn't He?"

After all, if He's supposed to be all-powerful, He could have stopped this. If He's supposed to be all-loving, He could have protected my heart and spared me this pain. But He didn't. He turned away and chose not to. So how can I trust a God like that—a God who would let something like this happen in my life?

Have you ever said words similar to these—or at least thought them? Have you gotten to the place where being mad at your offender isn't quite enough for you anymore? In your search for answers and justification,

Do we ever have the right to be angry at God?

have you turned instead to wag your finger toward the heavens and let God have it for treating you the way He has? Or maybe it's not so blatant—more like a nebulous, simmering resentment.

Can such feelings and accusations ever be warranted? Does God condone such backtalk from the people He created? Does our relationship with Him include the privilege of being this honest in our expressions?

Do we ever have the right to be angry at God?

Believing the Impossible

Bill Elliff, who with his wife, Holly, has been a longtime friend, was a grown man before he endured the gut-wrenching blow of a parent's betrayal. Up until that time, he would have told you that his childhood years were almost embarrassingly ideal. Mom and Dad were the living portrait of love and commitment. His dad's service as a pastor and denominational church leader wasn't an act. Their ministry together was one of genuine joy and gratitude—enough to inspire all three of the boys to become preachers, and his sister to become a preacher's wife.

In fact, Bill was already out of seminary and well into his ministry calling, musing at times on how gracious God had been in his life, how little pain and trouble he and his family had been forced to face.

By this time, his dad had stepped away from weekly pulpit duties and had been providing expertise and oversight to a large group of churches in their denomination. When he finally approached retirement age, he had accomplished all his goals and more. He had lived a full life, with the rewards of his golden years ahead, ready to be shared with the wife of his youth—the wife he had been faithful to for more than four decades.

That is, until the roof caved in.

Through the harsh intervention of one man, Bill's father was denied a final important ministry assignment that he really desired. At that point, rather than receiving God's grace to deal with the disappointment, he allowed bitterness and unforgiveness to take root in his heart. In this state, he began to counsel a woman in his office who was struggling in a tough marriage.

Then this man, the one man you might easily have said was the last person on earth you'd ever expect this of, allowed himself to be lured into an immoral relationship.

Bill didn't know this right away, of course. The evidence of his dad's indiscretion sort of trickled down. Suspicions crystallized into realities that were hard to ignore or escape. Evidence mounted in the face of adamant denials. Finally, when it seemed they simply must know the truth, his grown siblings went to their parents' home unannounced, asked the hard, disbelieving question, and confirmed the painful truth.

So began a several-year roller-coaster ride of nauseating dips and turns. Here sat a precious wife and mother, who was dealing the most personally and painfully with this shameful act of betrayal and rejection. Yet even in the face of her husband's erratic swings of behavior and perspective, she remained steadfast in her desire to handle this matter God's way. She had been

wronged, yes. Cruelly, needlessly wronged. Yet she was choosing to let God comfort her heart. She was choosing to forgive.

For Bill, however, everything he had ever known or
believed—about life, about his dad, about his calling, about
God—was being riddled with unanswered questions.

"Why would God allow this to happen? Weren't we trying,
as a family, to serve Him? Why wouldn't God answer our
prayers—and answer them *now?* How could a loving God allow
His children to suffer so? Is God always true to His promises?
Or not?"

One day, deep into this seemingly endless ordeal, Bill's
mother returned from an everyday errand to find no one at
home, nothing but a carefully placed note on the table. In the
end it had come down to this—this final, pitiful excuse for a fit-
ting conclusion. Like the last page of a novel you kept hoping
would take a turn for the better, this one single piece of paper
gave sad, silent expression to everyone's most dreaded thoughts.

Dad was gone. With the other woman. And he wasn't coming back.

How Long, O Lord?

We'll return to Bill's story later on in this chapter, but I want
to pause to explore this quite natural reaction to pain and distress, this inclination to become angry and displeased with God
when we are harmed or injured by others.

I have come to believe that, at one level, all bitterness is ultimately directed toward God. It may be cloaked in anger toward a particular person or group of people who have wronged us, but it actually extends far beyond them, far above them.

We all seem to know intuitively that God's power is great enough to deal with our problems—if He wanted to.

So when woundedness turns to bitterness—when unforgiveness is given enough room, time, and oxygen to take on a life of its own—the prospect of a powerful God who doesn't seem to care enough about us to step into our situation is troubling to us. It goes against everything we've been led to believe about His goodness and fairness, everything we've painted in our minds about an even-handed God who always squares things in the end.

We even seem to be given a measure of permission to feel this way as we read the impassioned cries and prayers of the Psalms. You don't need a concordance to find them. The emotional transparency of these verses spills from nearly every turn of the page.

> *How long, O Lord? Will you forget me forever?*
> *How long will you hide your face from me? . . .*
> *How long shall my enemy be exalted over me?*
> (Psalm 13:1–2)

> *All this has come upon us,*
> *though we have not forgotten you,*
> *and we have not been false to your covenant.*

Our heart has not turned back,

  nor have our steps departed from your way;

  yet you have broken us in the place of jackals

  and covered us with the shadow of death.

Awake! Why are you sleeping, O Lord?

  Rouse yourself! Do not reject us forever!

Why do you hide your face?

  Why do you forget our affliction and oppression?

(Psalm 44:17–19, 23–24)

Job, too, was not afraid at times to take the gloves off in dealing with God's seeming injustice:

I would speak to the Almighty,

  and I desire to argue my case with God. . . .

Why do you hide your face

  and count me as your enemy?

(Job 13:3, 24)

How Far Is Too Far?

Can we be honest with God? Absolutely.

Are we not encouraged to have a righteous anger against sin, including the sins that have been committed against us? Yes, we are.

But there is a point where our honest questions directed

toward God cross the line and become an expression of a proud heart. Insubordinate. Demanding.

The Word cautions us against letting even righteous anger escalate into sin: "Be angry, and do not sin" (Psalm 4:4). Instead, the psalmist exhorts us to ponder these things "in your own hearts on your beds, and be silent. Offer right sacrifices, and put your trust in the Lord" (vv. 4–5).

God is God. We are not.

This is in many respects the basis for our relationship with Him. Beyond that, He loves you, cherishes you—and is doing something in the midst of this horrendous situation that might be hard to believe even if He wrote it across the heavens in clouds and smoke.

In His inscrutable wisdom and love, He is able to use even the most agonizing circumstances that touch your life in this fallen world to refine and purify you, to make you fruitful, and to magnify His grace and glory through your life. I know it's sometimes hard to believe. I know you may not see how you can possibly continue with this pain another week, another day, another hour.

But unleashed anger toward God comes, I believe, from having a faulty view of Him, from thinking that He is flippantly ignoring you, that He couldn't care less what you're going through.

The truth is, He is going through it with you and for you. I love that verse in Isaiah that so tenderly describes God's dealings with the children of Israel (even when they were reaping

the consequences of their own sinful choices): "In all their suffering, He suffered" (Isaiah 63:9 HCSB).

And in all your suffering, He suffers.

He is with you, right in the midst of it. Helping you. Loving
you. Hurting with you. Driving you back to Him, drawing you
closer in, making you more dependent upon His grace and power.

As you get to know and trust His heart, you will be able to
face the cross—the way Christ faced it from the haunting shad-
ows of Gethsemane—and still say, even through your tears,
"Not my will, but Yours be done."

Wonder-Whys and What-Ifs

Ruth's mother-in-law, Naomi, is a classic biblical example of
this very dilemma.

Have you ever watched your mate make a seriously unwise
decision, only to discover over time that *you* were the one who
would suffer the harshest consequences for it? Have you been
the one to pay the most, it seems, for someone else's mistake?

You can relate, then, to the fertile ground for bitterness in
Naomi's life.

During a time of famine in their hometown of Bethlehem,
her husband, Elimelech, made a shortsighted decision for their
family to go live "for a while" in Moab, just long enough for the
crisis to let up (Ruth 1:1 NIV). Unfortunately, "a while" turned
into many years. And before their plans of going back home
again could be realized, Elimelech died.

To make Naomi's homecoming even more unlikely, to drive her unwanted roots even deeper into pagan soil, her two sons chose to marry Moabite women. But in the ensuing years, tragedy struck again . . . and again . . . as both her boys died, leaving their young wives without husbands.

And Naomi without a family.

In the well-known story of her return to Bethlehem with her daughter-in-law Ruth, the Bible records the hometown reaction to this one who had gone away with her husband seeking fullness but had come back even emptier than before—not just empty in body now but empty in soul.

"Is this Naomi?" they asked each other. Was this the same woman who perhaps at one time had been so pleasant and happy, so vibrant and contented with her life as a wife and mother . . . before the days when her husband had led her away from everything that was familiar to her, chasing a foolhardy scheme to fix his family's problems? In the end—no matter how complicit she may have been in their relocation plans—she felt that his unwise decision had ruined her. As far as she was concerned, life was over.

"Do not call me Naomi," she said to them—a name which means "pleasant." Instead, "call me Mara [bitter], for *the Almighty* has dealt very bitterly with me. I went away full, and *the Lord* has brought me back empty. Why call me Naomi, when *the Lord* has testified against me and *the Almighty* has brought calamity upon me?" (Ruth 1:20–21).

Do you see who is getting the blame for her calamity? Naomi

and Elimelech had made a choice. If all had gone well, they would probably have patted each other firmly on the back for being sharp enough to outsmart the elements and to read their situation so correctly.

But all had *not* gone well. And God was taking the fall.

Have you been there? Have you found yourself the victim of your own poor choices or perhaps the poor choices of others? But instead of taking responsibility for them or choosing to forgive the one who misled or mistreated you, your ultimate response has been anger toward God for letting this turn of events occur without warning you, without bailing you out, without stepping in and stopping it while there was still time to avoid disaster?

It's at this point that some would even suggest a need to "forgive God"—as though He had erred and was in need of pardon. *Us? Forgive God?* Think about it. Even if said by a heart not meaning to offend or overstep, the very idea borders on outright blasphemy. To think we have that kind of power over the righteous, sovereign God is to demean His name and inflate our importance.

No, God doesn't need forgiveness from us. He is never guilty of making mistakes. In fact, the thing you may think is a cruel injustice on His part may actually turn out to be the best thing that ever happened to you. It can at least, we know—by the Father's all-wise grace—be transformed for your good, for His glory, and for the advance of His eternal kingdom.

So I ask you to look again into the heart of God and to see Someone who has a deeper, more loving plan for your life—

even in the midst of this painful turmoil—than you could ever figure out on your own. You can be confident that if you will choose to submit your way to Him through this trial of faith, His presence and provision will be sufficient for you. He will use this disappointment, this heartbreak, this unspeakable circumstance to teach you, train you, and fulfill His holy, eternal purposes for your life.

The alternative—anger with God—can do nothing but make things worse and further delay your healing.

What Do You Say?

Naomi didn't get that. Even the word she used for God in her outburst—*El Shaddai*, "the Almighty," the All-sufficient One—merely accentuated the depths of her anger and disillusionment. *Sure, you folks may call Him Almighty, All-Sufficient, Jehovah—all those high-sounding names you fool yourself into believing—but not me. He certainly hasn't lived up to His name in my life.*

A friend told me the other day about a recent conversation with her sister who has experienced some significant losses—and is sounding a lot like Naomi. A professing Christian, she feels God has turned His back on her and has failed to be who she thought He was; so she is living her own life, independent of God, and making decisions that are clearly contrary to His Word. Though she doesn't acknowledge it, her anger and bitterness have been turned toward God.

What about you? Do you feel that God has not lived up to His name in your life? Does it seem that He has been one thing in the sermons and the Sunday school lessons but quite another when you needed Him the most?

Listen to yourself. What are you saying about Him? What is your life communicating to others about Him?

All Naomi could do was talk about how awful God had been to her. But when people hear *you* speak His name, or describe His character, or resent the circumstances that have come into your life—what are they led to believe about Him?

I was moved by the letter that Pastor John Piper sent out to his many readers, listeners, and friends after his diagnosis with prostate cancer.[1] Even someone as biblically sound and steady as he is might not have reacted to that kind of news with grace and godly perspective.

But he did, of course. And his words inspired my heart, like the call of God across the vast span of eternity, reminding us to hold on through this temporary stretch of years we call a human lifetime, knowing that our Father in heaven is doing all things well.

After sharing the diagnosis, Dr. Piper went on to say:

This news has, of course, been good for me. [That sentence arrested me: "This news has . . . been *good* for me?" Was that a misprint? No . . . read on.] The most dangerous thing in the world is the sin of self-reliance and the stupor of worldliness. The news of cancer has a wonderfully blasting effect on both.

I thank God for that. The times with Christ in these days
have been unusually sweet. . . .

God has designed this trial for my good and for your
good. . . . So I am praying, "Lord, for your great glory, don't
let me miss any of the sanctifying blessings that you have for
me in this experience."

As I read those words, I thought, "This man really believes
what he preaches! And he is living it out in the midst of the
furnace."

Naomi's perspective was so different.

No question that she had suffered a great deal. She had been
forced to endure a lot of things that were probably not her fault.
But instead of running to God as her refuge, she responded to
Him in bitterness. And the evidence was all over her face.

It reminds me of the verse I've referenced previously—
Hebrews 12:15—about the "root of bitterness" that "springs up
and causes trouble, and by it many become defiled."

I've seen over and over again the damage that "Naomis" can
do—in a marriage, in a church, in a workplace, in a ministry, in a
friendship, in a family. Their bitterness, their anger toward God
and others, is toxic, though they are often the last to recognize
both their bitterness and the effect they have on others. In their
attempts to salve their wounds or to gain sympathy and understanding, they contaminate their corner of the world.

Our anger toward God will inevitably become a poison that
spreads far beyond our own hearts, just as it did with Naomi.

What seems so intensely personal becomes impossible to keep to ourselves. Believe me, it shows.

Unfulfilled Longings

Perhaps your anger with God stems from a dream He hasn't allowed you to realize—a promotion that went to someone else less deserving, a financial setback that's forcing you to live far below the standard of living you were once accustomed to.

Perhaps your anger with God comes from being single in a married world.

Childlessness, too, can be a source of anger against God. Why would He taunt any of us in this way, at such a vulnerable part of our hearts and lives? And yet we must learn how to accept what we receive—or don't receive—from Him. We must learn how to bow before His sovereignty.

It comes down to a choice: Blame God and rail against Him for His capricious cruelty, complaining and insisting on getting our way. Or trust that He knows what He's doing, that He is working in us to both purify and prepare us for lives of greater service and usefulness, and that He is employing one of His greatest teachers—time—in order to enlarge our hearts and expand our vision.

This is the hard work of Isaiah 26:3, the submissive discipline of keeping our minds "stayed" on the Lord, trusting Him in ways we cannot see or understand, in places where we must learn to be content with mystery.

Airline pilots have to learn how to read their instruments—and to trust those instruments. When they get into a storm or white-out conditions, they can get disoriented; their sense of direction gets turned around and can easily mislead them and cause them to make decisions that would endanger lives. In those situations, they have to make a conscious choice to believe the instruments, rather than their instincts or their feelings.

For believers, the Word of God is our instrument panel. There will be points in our lives when, in the midst of "white-out conditions," our feelings will betray us and contradict His Word—insisting God doesn't care or that He's made a mistake. At that point, we dare not rely on our feelings but must choose to trust that what the Instrument tells us is true.

We are born as people ruled by our emotions and feelings. But we "did not come to know Christ that way" (Ephesians 4:20 NIV). Part of being transformed into a new creation means that our feelings no longer get full, unquestioned access to our internal "driver's seat."

The longer I live under God's providence, the more readily I can trust Him when it comes to life's unsolved mysteries.

In this way, then, the lines that separate Christians and non-Christians begin to diverge. No wonder the unbeliever has little choice but to be angry with God when life mistreats him. His emotional outbreak has nothing bigger and more persuasive to check it, no steady, objective instrument from which to gain perspective and to direct his response.

But by our redemption—*by being forgiven*—we are empowered by His grace to submerge our hot, emotional, human anger beneath a legitimate trust in God's loving, eternal purposes for our lives.

The longer I live under God's providence, the more readily I can trust Him when it comes to my unfulfilled longings and life's unsolved mysteries. The more joyfully I am able to love and worship Him and to be satisfied with that which He supplies. And the more patiently I can wait for that day when faith will be sight and all that which made no sense to my limited frame of reference will be made clear.

Near-Death Forgiveness

Humanly speaking, Bill Elliff's mom had every reason to allow a root of bitterness to spring up in her heart, after the way her husband had sinned against her. Then, as if she hadn't already suffered enough, no more than a year after her husband left home, she contracted Alzheimer's. Another possible reason to be angry at God.

I can't imagine what that year had really been like for her.

(Perhaps you can.) But I can imagine that it would have been easier now than ever to resent what her husband's heartless actions had brought on—being forced to endure the slow, fearsome loss of her bearings and faculties without a loving, supportive husband to be there for her, to catch her when she was falling, to lower her risk of embarrassment, to keep her growing limitations from being quite so obvious and exposed for all the world to see.

Her marriage was gone. Her health was going next. What was left to trust God about?

One day Bill let himself into her nearby apartment, which the family had rented so he and his sister could keep a closer eye on her. It was quiet. Too quiet. And as he stepped into her room, he could tell something was wrong.

His mother was barely alive. Sweeping her into his arms, Bill rushed her to the nearest hospital, where doctors confirmed that she had suffered a cerebral hemorrhage. Before the afternoon was out, she had slipped into a coma; the doctors held out little hope that she would live through the weekend.

Yet a week later, she unexpectedly emerged from unconsciousness, uttering words that were unintelligible at first, forcing Bill and his sister to strain to make them out. Only one word was clear enough to be understood, and she repeated it three times.

Forgive . . . forgive . . . forgive.

The next day, as her family gathered around her bed—sometimes singing, sometimes praying, sometimes reading

Scripture or just sharing memories with their mom, who was now aware of what was going on—the phone rang.

It was Bill's dad.

The family put the receiver to their mother's ear . . . and listened as she strained to put voice to her words of forgiveness and love, the parting gifts of grace to this man who had wounded her heart but could not steal her trust in a gracious and good God. The next morning, as a brief window of lucidity opened for her to express what her whole being was feeling, she said to her son, "Billy, isn't it great about Dad calling? Why, this is what we've been praying for, that he would return to the Lord!"

He knows your heart. He has not left you alone.

Later that night, the curtain of unconsciousness fell around her face once again. For the next five weeks, she lay in a coma from which she would never return. A few days before her homegoing, her entire family gathered one last time around her bed—her sons, her daughter, their spouses, her grandchildren . . .

And her husband.

Bill's mom had realized early on in this ordeal that she would never be remarried to her longtime mate. She knew her life would never be the same, ever again. But as she struggled with her emotions and with the maddening effects of her unexpected, late-in-life trauma, she came to a point of surrender where she told the Lord, "All I want, Father, is for You to receive glory."

She could have chosen anger. That would have been only natural.

She could have shut God out and had no more use for what He offered. She probably had friends who would have agreed.

Instead, she gave herself to His purposes and was able to see them come to pass.

What about you? Are you in a place every bit as treacherous and untenable as Bill and his siblings and mom were? Have you wanted to scream your anger toward God through clenched teeth, banging on the doors of heaven that seem coldly closed to your heart and life?

Hear God asking the question He twice asked of His resentful prophet: "Do you do well to be angry?" (Jonah 4:4, 9).

He knows your heart, dear one. He has not left you alone. And by trusting in His sovereign wisdom, goodness, and love, you, too, may one day see the sweet restoration of everything you've prayed for.

But even if not, you will have found a refuge in His will and in His care—a blessed place that is reached only by those who trust His heart—and keep trusting it even when the darkness closes in around them.

Making It Personal

❋ Have you experienced some hurt, disappointment, or unful-filled longing that has caused you to question the goodness or wisdom or love of God? How have you responded?

❋ What does your typical response to adversity communicate to others about God?

❋ "Unleashed anger toward God comes from having a faulty view of Him" (p. 155). What steps could you take to develop a more accurate view of God and to deepen your trust in Him?

CHRISTIANITY DOES NOT MAKE LIGHT OF SIN. . . .
ON THE CONTRARY IT TAKES
THE SINS AGAINST US SO SERIOUSLY THAT,
TO MAKE THEM RIGHT, GOD GAVE HIS OWN SON
TO SUFFER MORE THAN WE COULD
EVER MAKE ANYONE SUFFER
FOR WHAT THEY HAVE DONE TO US.[1]

—*JOHN PIPER*

CHAPTER SEVEN

WHAT TRUE FORGIVENESS IS— AND ISN'T

I hope in the course of reading this book, the Lord has truly spoken to your heart about the importance and imperative of forgiveness. As you've thought back through the specific situations where forgiveness has come the hardest in your life, I pray that you have seen not only the depths of your sin that God has forgiven for Christ's sake, but also the deep well of His grace that can even now supply you with everything you need to show mercy to others.

It's there—*He's* there—if you choose to forgive.

It's possible that even after reading the Scriptures and examining the concepts we've explored, you still find forgiveness too painful and difficult to contemplate. Or perhaps, truth be known, you'd rather keep nursing your wounds and savoring your resentment than to release the offense. Either way, you're just not ready to forgive. If that's the case with you, I feel compelled to share a loving, but earnest, word of warning.

Your unwillingness to trust and obey God in this matter—even if it's more from exhaustion and self-preservation than from rank hardness of heart—will keep the atmosphere of your life contaminated with the poison of bitterness. You may not be conscious of its noxious effects every day, but it will cut off the flow of God's grace into your life. Satan will use it as a foothold to gain advantage over you, to point his finger of blame as evidence that you're not all you profess to be—and that God is not as strong and loving toward you as you'd like to think He is.

Forgiveness can't be proven by our feelings.

This doesn't mean that what's been done to you isn't terrible. But there is simply no comfort in unforgiveness. It soothes nothing. It takes you nowhere. Why go on letting it eat you alive when God's strength is so near at hand, so ready to bring you relief?

Having said that, I realize that many people who genuinely want to find themselves on the other side of forgiveness have bought into myths and misconceptions that have defeated their best attempts at following through. They have misunderstood what forgiveness should look like, feel like, and be like. As a result, they've found their journey to freedom frustrated.

In this chapter we'll look at four common myths that masquerade as truth in the area of forgiveness. There are others, of course, but these seem to be some of the most widely believed and among the most confusing. If you have fallen prey to any of these misunderstandings about forgiveness, as the light of His Word dispels the fog, you will be able to walk into God's open air with your head held high, your arms supported by His awesome strength, and your heart beating with gratitude for His abundant grace in your life.

This Doesn't Feel Like Forgiveness

Perhaps you've been misled by this common assumption— (1) *that forgiveness and good feelings always go hand in hand.*

You may have honestly, genuinely trusted God to help you forgive your offender. You've given Him your heart, you've laid it all out before Him, you've released the right to punish one who hurt you. But then the phone rings. Their birthday rolls around. A situation flares up where they handle a similar set of circumstances in the same insensitive way.

And your emotions start to heat up again.

That's when many people conclude, "I guess I haven't really forgiven him, because if I had, I wouldn't still feel this way."

But forgiveness can't be proven by our feelings, any more than it can be motivated or empowered by them. Forgiveness is a choice. And feelings often aren't. It's quite possible to forgive someone in totally the right way—God's way—and still have thoughts flash across your mind that completely contradict the decision you made.

In many ways, forgiveness is not rocket science. The imperatives of it—though often difficult to concede and comply with—are fairly straightforward as they're presented to us in the Scripture.

But neither is it an *exact* science. Forgiveness is not like planting tulip bulbs, where once it's done you never have to think about it again, and everything just comes up pretty and refreshing in the spring. Instead, life goes on and sometimes old feelings turn up when you're not watching, dug up to be handled and replanted, left on your doorstep to be dealt with all over again.

But that doesn't negate what you've done. It simply gives you an opportunity to let Him rule over those emotions, to stay the course and keep on forgiving—by faith.

Can't We Just Forget It?

Many people also live with this myth—(2) *that forgiveness means forgetting*. They'll point to what the Scripture says about the way God has forgiven us, how He has flung our sins "as far as the east is from the west" (Psalm 103:12).

But the Bible never says that God "forgets" our sins. How could a God who knows everything forget anything? Instead, the Bible says that He has not "counted" our sins against us (2 Corinthians 5:19). He has chosen not to remember them against us (Hebrews 10:17), not to bring them back up, never again to accuse or condemn us with them. He has modeled for us the silent promise of forgiveness.

So the fact that you have not been able to *forget* the offense doesn't necessarily mean that you haven't *forgiven* it.

We may be tempted to think how wonderful it would be if we could just forget all the pain—how much easier to forgive, if we didn't have to deal with all the memories. We could all wish that

The memory of past hurts can provide a powerful platform for ministry to other hurting people.

God would just take that divine eraser of His and in one fell swoop purge from our minds all those negative images of the past. Right?

I'm not so sure. I have discovered that the most stinging memories from the past can be powerful reminders of the grace and forgiveness of God, living monuments of His mercy in my life—markers that keep me dependent and trusting.

Further, the memory of past hurts can provide a powerful platform for ministry to other hurting people.

If we had no memory of how it feels for our hearts to be exposed and laid bare, damaged by the blows of sin and injustice, how in the world could we ever understand the pain that people around us are going through? How could we possibly be tenderhearted and compassionate toward them? And how could we reach out to them with His comfort in any sort of meaningful way—if we could not identify at least to some measure with suffering's sting?

Those memories help us realize how easy it can be for someone to find herself consumed with anger and sinking in desperation. They give us the ability to look others in the eye and say, "I've been there. I know. And I'm telling you, His grace is sufficient for you."

The Scripture reminds us that affliction not only allows us to receive deep, rich comfort from God but gives us a basis from which to minister that comfort to others:

The Father of mercies and God of all comfort . . . comforts us in all our affliction, so that we may be able to comfort those who are in any affliction, *with the comfort with which we ourselves are comforted by God*. (2 Corinthians 1:3–4)

This is so important. Forgiveness is far more than just a way for us to "cope" with our own wounds. The mercy and grace of God and the lessons learned along the way are intended to extend beyond us and be a means of blessing to others.

What God has invested *in* us is not just *for* us.

Thank God, of course, that He mercifully chooses to keep some things eternally withdrawn from our memory banks. But thank Him, too—as He gives you the grace to do so—that He chooses to leave behind enough to make us useful in ministering to others.

If we could totally forget, we would too easily become self-absorbed and useless. And deep down, we know it.

Forgiveness as a Process

There's a third myth that keeps many people from experiencing the reality and blessings of forgiveness in their lives— (3) *that forgiveness requires a long, drawn-out process and cannot take place until healing is complete.*

I have heard people say, "I'm moving toward forgiveness," or "I'm in the process of forgiveness"—sometimes even after years of counseling or therapy. There's no question that for some people, coming to grips with the awful offenses they've been forced to endure can be a long and arduous journey. The road just to get to the place where forgiveness is barely palatable is often a story in itself.

But I'll just say this from experience: I've watched believers "working their way" toward forgiveness for years and years and never getting there. In fact, I might even go so far as to say that when forgiveness is seen primarily as a work in progress, it seldom becomes a work in practice.

The choice to forgive does not have to involve a long, extended process—any more than God's forgiveness of *us* is a slow-moving, wait-and-see, not-till-I'm-good-and-ready series of events and checkpoints.

Now, the outworking of restoration and reconciliation in a broken relationship may extend over a period of time, requiring a lot more in the hard work department than one single prayer or decision. And as you grow in your understanding of the circumstances that took place, as well as your understanding of God's ways, the forgiveness in your heart may well go to deeper levels.

But *by God's grace, you can choose to forgive in a moment of time,* to the level of your understanding at that point. And though much more may be required of you down the line, the reality of being released from the prison cell of your own unforgiveness can happen today. This moment. An established fact.

Some would suggest that forgiveness should take place as the result and at the tail end of a lengthy healing process. While it's true that the healing of mind, emotions, heart, and relationships generally takes time and involves a process of growth, if we wait to forgive until we are fully restored, we will likely never forgive.

I believe that, as a rule, the *point* of forgiveness is followed by a *process* of healing and restoration—not the other way around. The willingness to forgive is often the beginning of true healing taking place. Coming to the point of forgiveness allows us to fully enter into the process of restoration.

Just as you were extended *God's* grace in a moment of time, you can extend grace to others as a right-now expression of your will. And then, as you mature in Christ, the fruits of forgiveness begin to blossom. Your heart grows more tender. Your words lose their edge of anger. Your responses become less quick and reactionary, more kind and gentle.

So although we do indeed make *progress* in forgiveness, it is not a *process* that has to be worked up to. It happens—then it grows on us.

Future Forgiveness

One final myth that needs to be exposed is this—(4) *that forgiveness should always make things better.*

Part of being human, made in the image of God, is the expectation that life should normally follow an upward trend, getting richer and fuller and more fulfilling along the way. That's why moviemakers craft stories that build in intensity and grow toward a thrilling climax. That's why the people who create the rides at amusement parks build their roller coasters to start slow and finish fast. That's why concerts and fireworks displays have a "grand finale."

But life generally isn't like that in our fallen world. Yes, for believers in Christ, who know that the years we spend on this earth are but a small fraction of our eternal lifetime, we are assured that there is a forever finale awaiting us in glory.

But in the meantime—if we're going to live at peace with God and our fellowman—forgiveness is going to have to be a way of life. As you have been wronged in the past, so you are certain to face future situations where you will again be wronged, maligned, and treated unfairly.

Over and over again in life—in your marriage, with your children, in the workplace, at church, even serving in a ministry—you will be faced with the same crossroads: do you forgive, or do you harbor resentment and bitterness?

Recently in my quiet time, I was meditating on the book of 2 Timothy—the letter that most scholars agree was the last written by the apostle Paul from prison, shortly before his execution. Even at that point, so late in his life—after years of faithful service for the Lord—Paul found himself dealing with fresh wounds.

Fearful of reprisals under Nero's repressive regime, "all who are in Asia turned away" from Paul (1:15). Then there was "Alexander the coppersmith," who had seriously undermined his ministry. This man caused Paul "great harm" (4:14) and was perhaps gloating over seeing him put away in prison.

There were others who had once been supporters of the gospel and friends of Paul's unique calling and ministry, but when the cost of friendship had gotten hot, requiring courage to go along with their convictions, "no one came to stand by me." All of them "deserted me." But the apostle's reaction to this kind of stinging disappointment was clear: *"May it not be charged against them"* (4:16).

How was he able to do it? How was he able to forgive . . . and to keep on forgiving even new hurts and offenses?

How do you do it when a freshly hired co-worker seems to delight in questioning your capabilities? How do you do it when your husband's longtime, secret obsession with online pornography suddenly comes to light, hitting you full in the face with the utter rejection and betrayal of it?

Or perhaps it's something much less severe and much more everyday. How do you forgive the neighbor whose dog barks half the night and wakes you up with frustrating regularity? How do you show mercy to the friend who turned an issue you shared with her in confidence into a prayer request for her small group?

Getting in the Habit

I think Paul derived this ability from at least three good habits he had honed over the years—two that are mentioned specifically in this passage in 2 Timothy, and another that seems to rest just beneath the surface.

(1) *Paul exercised total confidence in God's power and His eternal plan.* He wasn't oblivious to what was happening to him or around him. He didn't live in blissful denial or even try to "forget"

the things that had been done to him. Instead, he dealt with the blows by letting them marinate in this truth: "The Lord will rescue me from every evil deed and bring me safely into his heavenly kingdom" (4:18). He knew that those like Alexander who had done him harm, had more than Paul to deal with: "The *Lord* will repay him according to his deeds" (4:14).

When you are feeling overwhelmed by your inability to cope with the pain you feel, when your mind is being badgered with clever comebacks you wish you could use on your offender, when the strain of it all is more than you can bear, deliberately cast your cares upon the Lord. Turn your weakness into prayer. Throw yourself fully on the grace of God, and trust Him to handle this in His own way, in His own time.

(2) *Paul was more concerned about his calling than his comfort.* He knew that the proclamation of the gospel—the driving force of his life's work and energies—was more important than whatever drama was unfolding in his personal life. He recognized that the Lord's strength was not designed solely for his own benefit but "so that through me the message might be fully proclaimed and all the Gentiles might hear it" (4:17).

Does God have strength enough for you? Absolutely. He is able to rescue you "from the lion's mouth" and set you free from the suffocating grip of unforgiveness, just as He was for Paul. But He has more in mind for you than just seeing you happy and contented. His plan, His passion for transforming people through the power of the gospel is your calling, as well. And the story of your forgiveness will be one way He does that.

(3) *Paul had learned the secret of forbearance.* This is not a word we hear a lot today, but if we will learn how to practice it on a daily basis, it can become one of our greatest weapons in staving off unforgiveness.

To "forbear" means to show restraint, to be patient in the face of provocation, to be longsuffering and willing to put up with people's actions or inactions—to let things go.

Forbearance is actually a by-product of love, the kind of love that "covers a multitude of sins" (1 Peter 4:8)—or as Paul put it so eloquently in 1 Corinthians 13, a love that "is not provoked . . . does not take into account a wrong suffered . . . bears all things, believes all things, hopes all things, endures all things" (vv. 5, 7 NASB).

Let's look at it in real life:

- 🌸 Your husband fails to notice something special you did for him.
- 🌸 Your adult children don't call as often as you'd like.
- 🌸 Your boss blames you for something a co-worker did.
- 🌸 Your mother-in-law says something that hurts your feelings.
- 🌸 Someone walks right by you at church without saying a word.
- 🌸 It's obvious your parents think you're crazy for having another child.
- 🌸 A guy at church asks you every week, "Found a job yet?"
- 🌸 A motorist talking on his cell phone nearly runs you off the road.

What do you do? You forbear. You *let it go.*

Yes, some offenses need to be confronted and dealt with. But many others—most of them, in fact—just need to be overlooked and put away. (Our problem is, we tend to confront the sins we should overlook, and overlook the sins we should confront!)

The lack of forbearance in our homes and everyday circumstances causes us to exaggerate offenses—"until a [fly's] egg becomes as huge as ever was laid by an ostrich," as Charles Spurgeon put it.[2] It magnifies tension and intensifies conflict; it erects walls in relationships, makes us petty and peevish, and severs friendships. I'm convinced that many divorces could be averted if one or both partners would simply practice the grace of forbearance. Many tensions and misunderstandings in the workplace would vanish if we would learn to be forbearing with one another.

Exercising forbearance in minor matters is important practice for extending forgiveness in the bigger issues.

Exercising forbearance in minor, daily matters is important practice and preparation for extending forgiveness in the bigger issues that are sure to arise.

When we hear or read the stunning accounts of forgiveness that happen in the lives of ordinary people who have been thrust into extraordinarily stressful circumstances, it's doubtful that they suddenly developed this huge capacity to forgive. I think it's probably because all along they've been practicing forgiveness and forbearance in the everyday, spilled-milk situations of their lives.

The woman who forgives the man who raped her and left her not only pregnant with his child but infected with HIV, yet who says, "Every time we feel the pain, we need to forgive again"—

The man who watched his father shot dead over the few dollars in his wallet, but who one day shakes that same attacker's hand and declares, "I forgive you, and it's over"—

The mother who is hit head-on by a speeding, unlicensed driver, killing her two children and leaving her in critical condition, but whose first words to her husband upon reviving from a drug-induced coma are, "Did you forgive him?"—

These heroics don't just happen. Instead, they are almost always borne out in people who knew what it was like to forgive long before the stakes became life-changing.

And you can be one of those people, too.

Fifty Years Ago

As I was writing this book, the Christian world commemorated the fiftieth anniversary of the martyrdom of five missionaries slain by the Auca Indians (now known as Waodani) in the jungles of

Ecuador. The name most of us first think of in regard to this event is Jim Elliot, whose widow, Elisabeth, became such a dear part of many of our lives through her writing and speaking ministry.

Around the time of the anniversary, I had a chance to talk with Steve Saint, whose father, Nate, was also among those martyred along the South American riverbank that tragic afternoon. He took me back to those somber days and left me with some thoughts and impressions I won't soon forget.

Perhaps you can relate to losing a parent at a young age. I can only try to imagine what that level of heartbreak and fallout would be like. When Marge Saint told her five-year-old son that his dad wasn't coming back, he felt, of course, the incredible sadness almost unique to that kind of loss.

But when I asked Steve, fifty years later, if he had ever struggled with bitterness toward his father's killers, he responded: "I took my cues from my mom and the four other widows. I never, ever, heard any of them even suggest that God may have made a mistake—or that *they* had made a mistake." These women modeled a depth of godly trust that was evident even to their young children.

In fact, in creating the screenplay for a feature movie version of the story, the script writers insisted on showing Steve's anguish and anger, the way they imagined they themselves would have felt in the face of such personal tragedy. At one point, Steve said, he protested, "Guys, that wasn't real. I never hated these people. I never wanted to get even."

To which they responded, "We know that's true, Steve, but

only because your mom and these other women and your grand-parents all trusted God. You had a heritage of this, but most people in the world don't have that."

In reflecting on that exchange, Steve said to me. "I think they're right. But the reality for me was, I didn't know why the Waodani had done it, and I didn't know how I would grow up to be a father myself without a father to show me how, but I believed that God would make a way and that He had a plan. And fifty years later, I still think He has a plan."

It's astounding. The power of forgiveness. The power of those young widows' faith, which so easily and understandably could have been swallowed whole in self-pity, instead was used of God to shield their children from carrying armfuls of man-made baggage into the next generation.

We bear that kind of responsibility to our children and to others who are watching the way we live. What kind of legacy are you leaving for your children—and their children? If they take their cues from the way they see you respond to pain, disap-pointment, and loss, how will *they* respond to life's tragedies? How are your responses shaping their view of God? Have you considered the impact that your forgiving spirit (or your bitter-ness) will have on future generations?

Senseless Tragedy?

Amazingly, some of those widows and their families re-turned to the jungle to minister to the very ones who had carried out the massacre, and were used as instruments to bring the gospel to those who had wielded the spears and cruelly ended the lives of their loved ones.

Years later, one of the very men who had killed his father would have an opportunity to minister to Steve when he faced a crisis of a different sort.

Steve's daughter Stephenie—the youngest of their four children—had just returned from a year of touring as a keyboard player for a music group with Youth For Christ. Though not initially enthusiastic about the idea, Steve had ultimately given his blessing for Stephenie to take the year off from college, with the knowledge that she bore a missionary legacy—a passion not to be easily argued with. He and his wife missed their daughter terribly, wondered about the risks she was facing, and were greatly relieved the day she finally walked off the plane, home at last.

Their little girl was back.

During her "welcome home" party, she slipped away to her bedroom, complaining of a headache. At some point, her mother, Ginny, got Steve's attention to say that Stephenie was hurting pretty badly and wanted him to come pray with her.

Thankful (actually) for a chance to be alone with just his wife and daughter, he hurried to her room. Ginny was holding Stephenie on her lap like a little girl. Steve put his arms around them and prayed that God would take Stephenie's headache away.

While he was praying, he heard a little scream coming from

his daughter. He looked into her face and saw her eyes roll up into her head. She was having a massive cerebral hemorrhage.

By the time they got her to the hospital, she was dead.

"I didn't know what was going on," Steve said. "Even I just sort of had the idea that if we do what God asks us, then He's obliged to play by our rules. I know that isn't true, but it's tempting to believe that."

It was tempting, too, for Mincaye—the friend who stood beside Steve and Ginny at the hospital, the man who many years before had thrust the murder weapon into Nate Saint's body. "Who's doing this?" he was asking. "Why is she dying?"

But when the reality of it all began to drape down around them, this warrior from the Amazon jungle—who at first had wanted to defend Stephenie from the medical team and the ambulance, from sights and sounds he couldn't understand—was the first to give voice to what would become their greatest reassurance. "This is *God*," he said. "Don't you realize God Himself is doing this?"

"And in that moment," Steve shared with me as I wiped away the tears, "while the life of my only daughter, whom I loved dearly with all my heart, was draining away, Grandfather Mincaye, the man who killed my father, put his arms of faith around me and helped me hold on to that legacy I had received and to pass it on to the next generation. We don't always understand, but God has His reasons."

Total trust. Coming full circle. And all because of five brave women who dealt with unspeakable circumstances in God's way

—and whose legacy continues to yield God's kind of results.

Who could have imagined the scope of divine purpose that lay in that original atrocity, the day the war whoop echoed with death along a small inlet of the Ecuadorian jungle? Yet how many have been brought to faith, or moved to missions, or inspired to lifelong attitudes of grateful sacrifice because of five men who lost their lives in such senseless—senseless?—fashion.

No, we cannot begin to fathom God's purposes, even when they're happening right around us. But we can know that He *has* one and that His desire is to use us as part of its generations-long fulfillment.

If we will trust His heart. If we will forgive.

Making It Personal

 Identify any of the four "myths" addressed in this chapter
that have kept you from extending full forgiveness.

 Have you learned the secret of forbearance? What situations
are you facing currently where you need to exercise forbearance?

 What kind of legacy are you leaving for the next generation
in relation to forgiveness?

FORGIVENESS UNLEASHES JOY. IT BRINGS PEACE.
IT WASHES THE SLATE CLEAN.
IT SETS ALL THE HIGHEST VALUES
OF LOVE IN MOTION.
IN A SENSE, FORGIVENESS IS
CHRISTIANITY AT ITS HIGHEST LEVEL.[1]

—*JOHN MACARTHUR*

CHAPTER EIGHT

RETURNING A BLESSING

Mitsuo Fuchida was the lead pilot of the Japanese attack on Pearl Harbor—a fearless, expert flier specially chosen for this commanding role, the one who actually gave the order—Tora! Tora! Tora!—to the 360 fighter planes poised at his flank.

He called the killing of 2,300 American sailors "the most thrilling exploit of my career."

But what most people don't know is that in 1949,

less than eight years after the raid on Pearl Harbor, this dive-bombing daredevil came to faith in Christ.

God used two remarkable events to bring about this "unlikely" conversion.

The first came shortly after the war, while Fuchida was speaking to a friend who had been among those captured and detained in the United States. Curious to hear how the Americans had treated their prisoners, he listened to his friend tell of an eighteen-year-old volunteer who had consistently cared for and ministered to the needs of the Japanese. When the prisoners had asked why she was being so helpful to them, she said—unexpectedly, illogically—"Because Japanese soldiers killed my parents."

The young woman's mom and dad had been missionaries in Japan during the escalation of international hostilities that led to World War II. Judged to be spies, they had been beheaded after fleeing to the Philippines. Their daughter—not hearing this until three years later after being evacuated to the States—had naturally reacted to the news with bitter grief and anger. But knowing her parents, she ultimately came to the conclusion that they would have forgiven their killers. She just knew it. Therefore, she must forgive them, too. Not just forgive, but return blessing. And that's why she was there, she said—in the camps, loving her enemies.

This notion astounded Fuchida. How could anyone respond to her parents' murder in this way?

Then one day several years later, he was handed a small leaflet while waiting at a railway station. He probably would have tossed it, but the fact that it was written by a fellow aviator piqued his interest. Sergeant Jacob DeShazer's *I Was a Prisoner in Japan* was the first-person account of an American pilot who had been forced to parachute from his plane during the Doolittle Raiders' bombing of Tokyo, in retaliation for Pearl Harbor.

DeShazer was quickly captured by the Japanese military. He described his next three years as an endless nightmare of torture and starvation, frequent executions that took the lives of his fellow detainees, and solitary confinement that compressed his world into square feet—but inflamed and enlarged his hatred.

Two years into his imprisonment, however, he had been handed some books to read in the dim glow of his holding cell, among them a Bible. Like light in the darkness, the Word penetrated his heart—especially the verse that spoke so specifically to his present situation: "Love your enemies."

Changed by God's grace, DeShazer began deliberately speaking respectfully to his captors, even when their treatment of him was cruel

> *Forgiveness requires that we go "above and beyond" just releasing our offender.*

and degrading. "I prayed for God to forgive my torturers," he wrote in the leaflet, "and I determined by the aid of Christ to do my best to acquaint these people with the message of salvation."

Fuchida read DeShazer's story with amazement, then hurried to find a Bible he could buy, to see for himself where this strange command—"Love your enemies"—really came from.

The story ends with Fuchida coming to Christ, becoming an evangelist, and even teaming up with DeShazer to speak to large crowds throughout Japan and Asia, leading both men to friendship and many to salvation.[2]

And all because of two people who hadn't stopped with forgiveness but who had gone "above and beyond"—two people who had received harm and reciprocated with love.

Sealing the Deal

I've talked with people who believe they've truly forgiven their offender—they've pressed the delete key—but they still feel stuck emotionally. When they think of that person, they still feel tied up in knots. They've not been able to move forward with any kind of peace or freedom. Something's still holding them back.

God's Word gives us an important key to going all the way with forgiveness. It requires that we go "above and beyond" just releasing our offender—that we extend the grace of God and build bridges of love by returning blessing for cursing, good for evil.

But I've forgiven him! I'm not holding a grudge. I applaud you for taking the courageous step of releasing your offender(s) from the grip of your own anger and vengeance.

But there's more . . . God wants you to live in the kind of freedom that radiates His light and love from your smile to your handshake to the very soles of your feet.

True forgiveness goes a lot further than just saying, "I've forgiven him." As 17th century Puritan pastor Thomas Watson put it:

> *When do we forgive others?* When we strive against all thoughts
> of revenge; when we will not do our enemies mischief, but
> wish well to them, grieve at their calamities, pray for them,
> seek reconciliation with them, and show ourselves ready on all
> occasions to relieve them. This is gospel-forgiving.[3]

That's quite a standard! We are called to forgive others *as God has forgiven us.* How has God forgiven us? He didn't just say to us, "You're forgiven." He gave His Son's life for us when we were His enemies. Pursued us when we wanted nothing to do with Him. Adopted us into His family. Made us joint-heirs with Christ. Has promised never to leave or forsake us. Comforts us and meets our needs. "Daily loads us with benefits" (Psalm 68:19 NKJV). That kind of extravagant, undeserved grace models the way we are to forgive.

To forgive someone throws open the blinds and raises the windows, letting the fresh breezes of God's grace begin its healing work. But when we take the deliberate step to bless our offenders—to love our enemies—we are able to enter into the full power of forgiveness.

I come back to Gracia Burnham to illustrate this powerful principle. I introduced her story earlier in the book, how she and her husband endured the horrifying ordeal of being taken hostage and mistreated for months on end in the Philippine bush.

In her book *To Fly Again*, Gracia tells of one of their captors, a young man they called "57" because of the M57 rocket launcher he always carried as they set out on their marches. He was always sullen, always cranky, always arguing and looking like he was ready to bite their heads off. They never knew what he was going to do next and what they might possibly do to keep from so easily offending him.

But Gracia's husband, Martin, discovered one day that "57" suffered from serious headaches, which probably was what brought on most of his touchy reflexes. So Martin began offering him pain relievers from their small stash of medicines and other crude provisions.

"The fellow's attitude toward Martin changed instantly," Gracia remembers. "From that moment on, my husband was his friend."[4]

Such a simple act. An observant question. An aspirin. Yet to go there required that Martin get past a million rational reasons for not just being unconcerned about the bad-tempered man's headache, but secretly wishing he could give *all* his captors a serious headache!

Yet listen to Gracia's words, on this side of her cruel captivity, on this side of seeing her husband killed as a result, on this side of being cheated out of everything life was supposed to be for her: "To this day, I have a warm spot in my heart for that young man because of what Martin did for him."[5]

Closure. Capping it off. Being able to walk into the next day unhindered by the need to fight back and seek revenge.

There's simply no reason in the world, even when thinking in terms of the most crippling situations you've faced—"unforgivable" situations, to hear some of us talk—why you can't participate with God in obtaining full, complete, and conquering victory.

But to do so, you're going to have to take seriously—and literally—everything God says about it. Which includes something that may seem unthinkable: *blessing your offenders.*

As I suggested in the last chapter, God often chooses to leave behind some of the painful memories, the lingering feelings and effects of past hurts, so we can be

God has never met a circumstance so dreadful that it can't be recast into a trophy of His mercy and grace.

merciful and compassionate toward those who are going through similar ordeals. This is actually a great privilege bestowed upon us by a God more loving than many expect Him to be, who has never met a circumstance so dreadful that it can't be recast into a trophy of His mercy and grace.

But having said that, I do not believe for a minute that you should have to live the rest of your life under the weight and burden of all these unresolved emotions. And the reason many of us are still there, the reason we haven't yet moved on to more complete healing in these areas . . . is because we've stopped short of actually blessing those who have wronged us.

We need to go on. We need to finish what God has started. For our good. For their good. For God's glory.

Rewriting Wrong

We find this principle of blessing our offenders spelled out in Romans 12—not as an optional add-on, not as a senior-level course for those on the advanced placement track of Christian living. This passage is for you. And for me. And for everyone who needs God's help to go all the way in forgiveness. Follow the progression:

First, "repay no one evil for evil" (v. 17).

The Word is so direct and unmistakable. Don't return the evil you've received from others, God says. That's *His* job:

Beloved, never avenge yourselves, but leave it to the wrath of God, for it is written, "Vengeance is mine, I will repay, says the Lord." (v. 19)

Okay, I get that part. We're not supposed to pay back evil for evil —vengeance is God's job, not mine.

But there's more—here's what we are supposed to do:

To the contrary, if your enemy is hungry, feed him; if he is thirsty, give him something to drink. . . . Overcome evil with good."
(vv. 20–21)

Don't miss the incredible power contained in this truth. Not only do we not have to be victims of the evil others inflict on us. We can actually *overcome* evil—with good!

I want you once again for a moment to go through the mental exercise of identifying your offenders, those who have caused you pain and loss, who have given you the hardest time in trying to let go and forgive. And as you think of them, I want you to back away far enough from the achy feelings that may even still resonate within you . . . and I want you to see that person as someone in need.

Because he is.

When that person hurt you—that mate, that boyfriend, that parent, that ex-spouse, that college roommate, that aunt or uncle, that stranger who came out of nowhere to mar your life—he revealed that he has a need. A need he or she misappropriated at your expense.

Do you want to fully experience the freedom of forgiveness? Ask God to show you the real need in your offender's life.

Then ask Him how He might want to use you to meet that need.

That's exactly what happened in the life of Joseph, which we looked at earlier. He was wronged by his brothers, wronged by Potiphar's wife, wronged by the fellow prisoner who had promised to help effect his release but who instead forgot all about him. Yet when Joseph reached the other side of his ordeal, when forgiveness had already become a matter of his heart, he set out to bless the very brothers who had gotten him into this mess in the first place.

I'm always amazed when I read how Joseph responded to the brothers who had injured him so deeply. He refused to return evil for evil. He wasn't going to play their game. But he didn't settle for simple non-retaliation (showing *mercy*)—that's hard enough. Instead, he went way "above and beyond"—by actively, intentionally reaching out to minister to their needs (extending *grace*):

> *"Do not fear; I will* provide *for you and your little ones." Thus he* comforted *them and* spoke kindly *to them.* (Genesis 50:21)

That's supernatural! That's the redeeming, restoring heart of Christ that reached out to us when we deserved God's wrath, and instead, lavished His grace on us.

That's the heart behind Paul's instructions to the Corinthians regarding a church member who had sinned grievously and was now in need of restoration: "*forgive*" him, "*comfort him*," and "*reaffirm your love* for him" (2 Corinthians 2:7–8).

Does that sound too hard in your case? It should. It is *much* too hard. If we were ever in need of the Holy Spirit to enable us to obey His Word, this is it. People who are trying to survive life without the aid of God's grace and salvation don't have a prayer of doing what these verses require.

But you do. Otherwise, Jesus could never have had any grounds for saying,

> Love *your enemies,*
> Do good *to those who hate you,*
> Bless *those who curse you,*
> Pray *for those who abuse you.* (Luke 6:27–28)

So hear me clearly—this is not something you can do. But it is something God can do through you. And if you want to move forward in the healing process, then once you've come to the point of fully forgiving them, of releasing them, of pushing that delete button, ask God to show you how you can invest back into the life of your offender, the very one who sinned against you.

It doesn't have to be spectacular. It may be simply using kind words to respond to hateful ones. It may be a specially prepared meal. Or the offer of doing one of those household chores you know she detests. Even a gift certificate to a favorite restaurant or love note tucked in the sock drawer.

Start there. See what happens, if not in him or her, then in you. And see where God directs you to go next, until you actually begin finding joy—His joy—in blessing someone who's treated you so badly. In so doing, you will overcome evil with good.

This is street-level obedience. Nothing could be more real, more effective, or more powerful—both for you and for the offender.

I watched that happen before my eyes in the life of a friend who had been deeply wronged by her husband. She knew she could not harbor bitterness in her heart, so she forgave him. She knew she could not retaliate, so, hard as it was, she refused to return evil for evil.

But the freedom in her spirit as well as the ultimate repentance and restoration in his life came when she determined to return good for evil—getting up at the crack of dawn each morning to fix him breakfast before he headed off for work, ironing his shirts, praying blessings on him, responding to his harsh outbursts with gentle words and seeking his forgiveness when she failed to do so.[6]

Each act of (undeserved) kindness served to drive a nail in the coffin of any bitterness she might have been tempted to indulge and simultaneously sowed a seed of grace in the heart of the man she hoped to see restored to Christ.

Such is the fruit of forgiveness that goes "above and beyond."

A Deeper Shade of Forgiveness

Depending on the nature and circumstances of your relationship with some who have wronged you, it may not be appropriate for you to reconnect face-to-face or to reestablish ongoing contact with them. As previously noted, that decision should be made in counsel with your pastor or another mature, godly friend who can help you navigate this safely and biblically.

But no matter who it is or what he's done, you can at least do this: you can pray for him.

I mean, really pray for him.

You may sigh and say, "I don't think I can pray for God's blessing on that man or that woman. . . . I don't even *want* God to bless them!" But I assure you, as you begin to do it anyway out of simple obedience to the Word of God, you'll discover what I've found to be true in my own life: you can't long hate someone you're praying for, someone you're asking God to bless and restore to a right relationship with Him.

Our main goal for our offenders should be their reconciliation, first and foremost with God and then, if possible, with us. We may be able to help bring about that ultimate objective by building bridges of love and blessing across the divide. Regardless of their response, how can we keep the walls up, refusing to seek their blessing and restoration—and then expect to experience free-flowing fellowship with God ourselves?

The Power of Calvary Love

We are not the only ones who are set free when we choose to forgive and bless those who have sinned against us. In God's great economy, we become instruments of His redemptive work—conduits of His mercy and grace—in the lives of those who are on the receiving end of that blessing. They are brought face-to-face with the reality of Calvary love—when they know they deserve just the opposite.

In the end, such unmerited, unexplainable measures may prove to be the means of bringing them to brokenness and repentance over their sin.

Recently I received an e-mail from a colleague who knew I was working on a book on forgiveness and was prompted to remind me of the impact in his life when his wife felt the blows of his betrayal and answered back with blessing.

To this day, he can recall as if it were yesterday the haunted look, the terror-filled expression in his wife's face when he first confessed to her the rampant immorality in his life. "She was so hurt," he wrote, "it was beyond comprehending. I will never forget the awful conversation we had."

But there is something else he still recalls, something that has proved to be even more powerful than the hurt—not only in his wife's life but in his own restoration: "One thing that sticks out in my mind now, nearly four years later, is the lack of recrimination and the absence of 'stabbing back' just to hurt me in return."

To be sure, she was devastated and "very, very angry." Humanly speaking, she had every right to be. But through it all—the loss of many of her dear friends, the turmoil in her own immediate family as a result of her husband's sin, and even going to work to replace his lost income—"she has *not once* spoken to me with bitterness, meanness, or rancor."

"I am amazed by it," he said. "I continue to be. I believe the incredible love and sacrifice of my wife is the reason we are still together today and I am serving the Lord again."

That heart to forgive didn't come easily for this woman. A couple weeks after the exposure of her husband's sin, she had to make a sixteen-hour trip. On the way home, she spent the entire time in prayer—crying out to the Lord, pouring out her heartache, praying for her husband and their children, and trying to determine whether she should leave her husband.

That trip proved to be a turning point. It was during that seemingly endless drive home that God reminded her of all that He had gone through for her—that *His* forgiveness had extended to her sin. In her heart, she knew God was giving her a choice: to respond in love and grace, as God had received her, or to refuse God's grace and become a bitter woman.

"Thankfully," her husband wrote, "she chose the latter. Because of that one choice, I am here today—restored, back in fellowship with God, my family, and others. It has not been an easy road. It has required hard discussions, intense accountability, and counsel from caring, godly people.

"But it has all been possible because my wife chose to

forgive. I cannot think about it without realizing once again the incredible grace and love of God. And I for one will be forever grateful."

I can't promise you that blessing your offender will result in that kind of "storybook ending." But I can pretty much promise you this: if you choose *not* to bless in return, you are almost certainly assured of never seeing the reconciliation your heart longs for.

I have seen God do the unbelievable as His children have been willing not only to forgive their offenders, but to step out and return good for evil. I often counsel women, "Believe it or not, if you'll let Him, God can actually fill your heart with deep love and compassion for that person you have hated for years!" And I have seen Him do just that.

Yes, it's a miracle of God's grace. It's a miracle you can experience—not just once, but over and over again, as you cultivate a heart of forgiveness—forgiving others, as He has forgiven you.

Making It Personal

- Ask God where He would want you to start in applying Luke 6:27–28 and Romans 12:20–21. Who is the "enemy" you need to bless? What are some appropriate ways you can meet his needs, invest in his life, extend the grace of God to him?

WHEN JESUS, NAILED TO A ROMAN CROSS,
PRAYED, "FATHER, FORGIVE THEM,"
HE WIELDED A WEAPON AGAINST
WHICH CAESAR HIMSELF HAD NO POWER. . . .
WHO CAN STAND UP TO
THE FORCE OF FORGIVENESS?[1]

—*ELISABETH ELLIOT*

THE POWER OF FORGIVENESS

Forgiveness is no easy undertaking. I know that. Even as I have been putting the finishing touches on this book, I have experienced a series of unrelated "offenses" —most of them relatively small, but each one difficult to swallow.

A couple of these injuries have hit me at particularly tender places, painfully resurfacing some difficult relationships and issues I had thought were in the past—like breaking a scab not quite fully healed.

In spite of the fact—or perhaps *because* of the fact—that I have spent the last several months immersed in the subject of forgiveness, I have found myself in an intense battle—my emotions and my flesh desperately wanting to harbor the hurt, nurse the wounds, and "punish" those who inflicted them, while the Spirit within me keeps gently insisting, "*Let it go! Forgive . . . forbear . . . press the delete button!*"

As I have wrestled with these matters, my heart has been haunted—hounded—by the words I have written on these pages. And in this fresh test, I have had to make a choice, tough as it is, to relinquish any right to hold on to the hurt or to be a debt collector. I have had to bow to God's sovereignty, accept each wound as a necessary, sanctifying gift, and receive His grace to choose the pathway of forgiveness. To do otherwise would be to sign my own prison sentence and would be a grievous offense against God, even more so in light of how much He has forgiven me!

Perhaps your journey through these pages has surfaced some difficult issues and emotions, reminding you again—as if you needed reminding—that forgiveness is indeed a costly endeavor.

It certainly was for Jesus. It remains so for us.

But I hope and pray that what really stands out in your mind, as it does in mine now more than ever, is the grace available to us through our relationship with Jesus Christ—ample and all-sufficient, complete in every way, pressed down and running over for those who are ready to walk out of the prison of bitterness, ready to lay down our arms and our resistance . . . ready to forgive others as we have been forgiven.

Indeed, unforgiveness can have a powerful hold on us, strong enough to push people away and keep them out there at a distance for years on end. We all know how strong its tug and pull can be. But the power of unforgiveness is power wasted, energy expended with little to show for all we've invested in it.

It is only the power of forgiveness that can truly keep us in the flow of God's will, at peace in the storm, carried along in the ever-advancing river of His eternal plans and purposes for our lives—going somewhere that means something.

We've seen the power of forgiveness to bring healing into the life of the *offender*—like the Pearl Harbor pilot, or the doctor whose medical mistake ended a woman's life prematurely.

We've seen the power of forgiveness to bring healing into the life of the *offended*—like Gracia Burnham, or the wife in the last chapter who could

> *Forgiveness is a mighty tool in the hand of an all-powerful God to bring healing all around. To every conceivable type of situation and relationship—past or present.*

have allowed her husband's wrong choices to destroy their marriage.

Forgiveness is a mighty tool in the hand of an all-powerful God to bring healing all around, to every conceivable type of situation and relationship—past or present.

In fact, forgiveness can have a long-lasting impact on *future* situations and relationships. As you choose the pathway of forgiveness, God may use your obedience to prevent sinful patterns and needless pain from being passed along to your children and to generations yet to come.

A friend recently sent me an e-mail in which he recounted some memories of his growing-up years. His mother had grown up with a mother who had a terrible temper that she never gained control of throughout her life. Following in the same steps, my friend's mother, though now a Christian and godly woman far along in years, likewise was an angry woman who frequently lashed out in anger toward her family.

For some reason, my friend's sister, Bonnie, had been the one to receive the worst of their mom's caustic fury over the course of her childhood. She grew up hating the ways she had been treated by her mother.

After Bonnie married and had her first child, she shocked herself one day when her little boy, who was under a year old, did something "wrong," and she found herself screaming at him in rage. Horrified, she realized that the anger of her grandmother and mother was now hers. It scared her—scared her to hear words she hated, words she had promised never to inflict on her own children, now coming out of her mouth with the same ease and volume. She fell on her knees and begged God to deliver her.

Some months later, she attended a conference where she heard a speaker talk about the importance of forgiveness. The speaker challenged her audience to treat past wrongs like a "record" (remember records, before tapes and CDs?)—rather than playing that record over and over again in their minds, she urged them, "Take the record of those wrongs and break it over your knee. Only then," she said, "will you be free and able to love the ones who wronged you."

Bonnie took those words to heart and, as an act of obedience and faith, "broke the record" she had replayed countless times in her mind—the record of her mom's angry outbursts and actions, of hurtful, humiliating words spoken to her as a child. By God's grace, she fully forgave her mom.

Not only did God heal the rift between Bonnie and her mother, but miraculously He broke that stranglehold of anger in her own heart and set her free—breaking a sinful pattern that had plagued three generations or more.

As my friend says of his sister, "Bonnie has been one of the most loving, wise, and godly mothers I've ever seen. She has not lashed out at her children in anger as her mother did to her. God brought this to an end—fully and permanently—when she came to the place where she forgave our mother—fully and permanently—for the wrongs she had committed against her.

"Bonnie would tell you today, as she has counseled many

women over the years, that forgiveness held the key to recovery and transformation in her life."

That's the power of forgiveness.

But we must never forget this—forgiveness is more than a way to find personal freedom, more than a way to ease the pain we feel in our hearts. It is even more than a way to hold out the hope of reconciliation to those who have wronged us.

In a sense all those benefits are secondary to an even higher outcome. The ultimate goal of forgiveness, just as the ultimate goal of our whole lives should be, is to bring *glory and honor to God*.

Forgiveness in the life of a believer showcases the astounding, redemptive heart of God. It puts on display the riches of His abundant mercy and His amazing grace, for all to see.

As I sit here at my laptop and think of all that we have considered about forgiveness in this book, the refrain of that great hymn by Samuel Davies (1723–1761) keeps ringing in my mind:

> Who is a pard'ning God like Thee?
> Or who has grace so rich and free?

That's what it comes down to. Forgiveness is not so much about us as it is about Him. Every opportunity you encounter to practice forgiveness is an opportunity to draw attention to the God who so delights to show mercy and to pardon sinners that He gave His only Son to make it possible. When those around you see you forgiving, when they hear your stories, when they watch for your reactions, they may be seeing Christ in a way they've never know Him before. And they may be drawn to love, worship, and trust that great "pard'ning God."

Forgiveness is not just an act of obedience for obedience's sake. Yes, we are commanded to forgive. And yes, we who have been forgiven so much certainly have no right to be debt collectors. But more than an obligation, forgiveness is a high calling—an opportunity to be part of something eternal, to shower back our gratitude to the One who forgave us everything (and you know what that "everything" entails for you).

Think of it as an offering, a sacrifice, a love gift to God . . . for Him and Him alone. If He adds to the blessing by causing our forgiveness to be of help to us or others, so much the better. But to know that He is pleased and praised—that is reason and reward enough.

Eternity's Anthem

To those who don't know better, forgiveness may seem like weakness—giving up, letting evil triumph, letting the "bad guys" win. In fact, at first blush, Calvary itself may seem to be just such a defeat—the prince of darkness trumps the Prince of Peace and renders Him helpless.

But seen from the vast reaches of eternity, the cross actually spelled Satan's ultimate defeat and proved to be God's greatest victory! "Sown in dishonor," Christ was "raised in glory"—"sown in weakness . . . raised in power" (1 Corinthians 15:43).

The Lamb of God lays down His life on the altar of sacrifice. As the last drops of His lifeblood are spilled out, He appeals to His Father to forgive those whose sin He bears. He draws— and expels—His final breath.

And all heaven breaks out into a mighty anthem: *Forgiven! Pardoned! Paid in full! Mercy granted! Justice vindicated! Redemption accomplished!*

Three days later, the Lamb slain for sinners from the foundation of the world is raised from the dead—the Lion of the Tribe of Judah.

And He shall reign forever and ever.

And we shall be before His throne—sinners made saints, enemies reconciled to God, clothed in the fine linen of His righteousness—to worship and serve Him day and night forever.

Such is the amazing, eternal power of forgiveness.

Making It Personal

❉ Is there a "record" you still need to break? By His grace, do it today.

❉ Worship God for His amazing forgiveness and grace.

NOTES

1. Duane W. H. Arnold, *Prayers of the Martyrs,* Comp., trans., (Grand Rapids: Zondervan, 1991), 108-109

Introduction

1. Leon Alligood, staff writer, *The Tennessean,* October 17, 2005, sect. A, pp. 1–2.

2. Charles Dickens, *Great Expectations* (Oxford University Press), 82.

3. John MacArthur, *Forgiveness* (Wheaton, IL: Crossway Books, 1998), 7.

Chapter 1: Walking Wounded

1. John Feinstein, *The Punch: One Night, Two Lives, and the Fight That Changed Basketball Forever* (Boston: Little, Brown, and Co., 2002), introduction.

Chapter 2: What Happens When We Refuse

1. Lawrence O. Richards, *New International Encyclopedia of Biblical Words* (Grand Rapids: Zondervan, 1991), 127.

2. Jordana Lewis and Jerry Adler, "Forgive and Let Live" *Newsweek,* September 27, 2004, 52.

3. Claudia Kalb, "End Your Back Pain," *Reader's Digest,* March 2005, 145.

4. Newsweek, "The Good Heart," October 3, 2005, 49–55.

5. "As We Forgive Our Debtors," message preached by John Piper, March 20, 1994 (www.desiringGod.org/library/sermons/94/032094.html).

Chapter 3: The Promise of Forgiveness

1. Pomegranate Productions, 2001, 124–25, 161–63.

2. God has ordained both civil and church authority to punish evildoers and to protect the righteous. It is possible to have forgiveness in your heart toward a mate or son or daughter or employer while still reporting their illegal behavior to the authorities God has established to deal with such offenses or appealing to the spiritual leadership of your church to confront the unrepentant person.

Chapter 4: Forgiving for Jesus' Sake

1. Life Action Ministries has four teams that conduct extended meetings in local churches, for the purpose of seeking God for personal and corporate revival. To learn more about Life Action or to inquire about scheduling a team in your church,

contact: P.O. Box 31, Buchanan, MI 49107; 800/321-1538; www.LifeAction.org; info@LifeAction.org.

2. Oswald Chambers, *My Utmost for His Highest*—November 19.

3. Ibid., November 20.

4. Ibid., November 20.

5. North American Review, January, 1834, cited in http://www.cyberhymnal.org/htm/t/f/tfountfb.htm.

6. Religion Today Summaries, Wednesday, June 22, 2005. Religion Today Summaries is a publication of Crosswalk.com, a Web site provided by the Salem Radio Network.

Chapter 5: The Art of Forgiveness

1. Gracia Burnham with Dean Merrill, *To Fly Again* (Wheaton, IL: Tyndale, 2005), 43.

2. Ibid., 43–44.

Chapter 6: Angry at God

1. John Piper, January 6, 2006 letter.

Chapter 7: What True Forgiveness Is—and Isn't

1. John Piper, *Future Grace* (Sisters, OR: Multnomah Press, 1995), 268.

2. C.H. Spurgeon sermon, "Forgiveness Made Easy," http://www.spurgeon.org/sermons/1448.htm.

Chapter 8: Returning a Blessing

1. John MacArthur, *Forgiveness* (Wheaton, IL: Crossway, 1998), 161.

2. "Glory from the Ashes," Focus on the Family (December 2001); "The Kamikaze of God," *Christianity Today* (December 3, 2001).

3. Thomas Watson, *The Lord's Prayer*, 252.

4. Gracia Burnham with Dean Merrill, op cit, 54.

5. Ibid., 54–55.

6. "Blessing" and "doing good" to her husband did not mean that she excused, overlooked, or enabled his sinful choices—genuine love required that she speak the truth, But she determined to do so without rancor, bitterness, or malice in her heart.

Afterword: The Power of Forgiveness

1. Elisabeth Elliot, *Love Has a Price Tag* (Ann Arbor, Mich., 1979), 48.

SMALL GROUP DISCUSSION GUIDE

As You Begin

There are no "magic" words or secret formulas for dealing with the hurt and pain we experience in this fallen world. But forgiveness is a powerful key that can set us free from being the prisoners of those who have wronged us. Though true forgiveness can be difficult to extend, God's Word shows us that it really is possible to break free from bitterness, regrets, and pain. That's the message of *Choosing Forgiveness*.

TIPS FOR GROUP LEADERS

Format and Structure

The purpose of this discussion guide is to help participants deepen their understanding of forgiveness and cultivate a forgiving heart and lifestyle.

This resource is designed to be used in a variety of contexts —from small groups to Sunday school classes. *Choosing Forgiveness* is broken into eight chapters, as well as an introduction and an afterword. That provides material for ten discussion sessions, which is how this discussion guide has been developed. (If desired, the study could be completed in eight sessions, by combining the Introduction with Chapter One and the Afterword with Chapter Eight.)

Depending on the best schedule for your group, you may choose to meet weekly or less often. Don't be in a rush to complete this study. Be sensitive if members in your group need additional time to digest and apply the material.

Encourage each member to read the chapter and to complete the "Making It Personal" section found at the end of most chapters, prior to your group meeting. If possible, they should also preview and be prepared to discuss the questions found in this discussion guide.

Be Sensitive

The whole subject of forgiveness implies the existence of offenses and relational issues. For most people, taking time to focus on this topic is likely to surface some pain and discomfort. Magnify that by the number of people in your small group, and you can see the potential for lots of soul-stretching growth. Don't fear the moments of discomfort—leave the Holy Spirit room to bring conviction and grace to the members of your group.

As members share out of their lives, you may hear expressions of bitterness and self-righteousness. Be a wise and sensitive listener. Before jumping in to correct, pray for your members and trust God to do the deep heart-work that is necessary on a topic like this. Most importantly, keep the gospel in clear view for the group. Your end goal for this study should be to see God form a group of grateful worshipers who know how much they've been forgiven and who are willing and committed to extend forgiveness to those who sin against them.

Ask God for grace to lead with wisdom and kindness. Ask Him to meet with each group member through the course of the study and to do whatever work is needed in each heart and life for the glory of His name.

Guidelines for Group Discussion

It may be helpful to establish some ground rules in your first meeting. First, confidentiality is important. Your members need to know that any relational issues that surface in the discussion will remain in the group. (An exception would be if there are issues that require the knowledge and intervention of church or legal authorities.) Here's a helpful boundary: If it's not your sin, then you have no reason to discuss the details with others. Let's be quicker to confess our own sins than the sins of others!

Second, this is a group discussion, not a confessional or a counseling session. If one of your members is struggling and needs extended personal ministry, invite her to meet with you at another time or suggest a meeting with your pastor or a wise, older woman. That way she can get the care she needs and your group will not get derailed from what God is doing in others' lives.

Third, enjoy your time together. Feel free to direct the discussion based on the size of your group and the allotted time. Avoid rabbit trails into secondary or unrelated issues. However, don't feel pressured to get through all the questions each time you meet. Depending on your available time and the size and openness of your group, you may end up only discussing two or three questions. The goal is not to get through all the content—the goal is for those in your group to encounter Christ and to grow in their understanding and experience of His amazing grace.

INTRODUCTION

Getting Started

As you begin this study, what are you hoping will take place as you read this book and participate in this discussion group? Share your thoughts with the group. (You may want to note now what you think you will gain from this study and reflect back on those thoughts when you come to the end of the study.)

Warming Up

Have someone read aloud the quote by Bishop Hassan Dehqani-Tafti, on the page before the Contents page. What makes this man's perspective so unusual?

Can you think of someone you have witnessed respond in a similar way to personal loss or suffering at the hands of another?

Can you think of any ways that your life has been enriched through some difficult or painful circumstance in your past?

Going Deeper

1. In Pastor John MacArthur's experience, *"nearly all the personal problems that drive people to seek pastoral counsel are related in some way to the issue of forgiveness"* (p. 29). Does that surprise you? What are some examples of common issues people struggle with that could relate directly or indirectly to a lack of forgiveness?

2. Discuss Regina Hockett's response to the murder of her daughter, Adriane. What observations stand out to you?

3. On page 23, the woman who was still reeling from her daughter's death at the hands of a stalker asks, *"How can I forgive?"* What are some reasons people struggle with the "how" of forgiveness?

4. How does the story of Miss Havisham illustrate the way many people respond when they are wronged? What are some ways people "close the drapes" and "stop the clocks" when they have been hurt? Can you relate to any of these responses at some point in your own life or in the life of someone you have observed? (Be careful not to share details that could put others in a negative light.)

5. *"If we are going to be true instruments of mercy in each other's lives, we must deal in truth . . . Sympathy can provide temporary relief, but nothing short of forgiveness can procure lasting release"* (pp. 24–25).

Can you think of a situation in which you were tempted to seek (or offer) mere "sympathy" toward someone who had been wronged, stopping short of the "truth" that they needed to extend forgiveness?

Share an example of someone who went beyond offering you sympathy when you had been wronged, and encouraged you to choose the path of forgiveness. What was the outcome?

6. Read and discuss Hebrews 12:15. What insights does this verse give us into the grace of God and the nature and results of bitterness?

7. *"For most of us, the problem isn't that we don't know about forgiveness. The problem . . . is either that we haven't recognized and acknowledged the unforgiveness that's in our hearts, or that we simply haven't made the choice to forgive"* (p. 28).

Invite members of your group to pray brief prayers aloud, asking God to open their own and each other's eyes and hearts to grasp more fully the message of forgiveness through the course of this study.

On Your Own

How well do you know what the Bible says about forgiveness? Before the next meeting, use the concordance in the back of your Bible to look up several verses on the topic of forgiveness (or bitterness). Be prepared to share anything that spoke to you from these verses the next time your group meets.

Grace Note

The promise of Hebrews 12:15 is that the grace of God is available to help you do the hard heart-work of forgiveness. You are not in this alone, wrestling with forgiveness in your own strength. This journey is entirely grace-based!

Chapter One:
WALKING WOUNDED

Getting Started

The theme of this chapter is summed up in the opening quote from Oswald Chambers: *"We talk glibly about forgiving when we have never been injured; when we are injured we know that it is not possible, apart from God's grace, for one human being to forgive another"* (p. 32).

Why is it important to acknowledge the wounds that sin leaves behind?

Since Last Time

Your assignment last time was to meditate on study various Scriptures about forgiveness. Which verse(s) particularly ministered to you—and why?

Going Deeper

1. *"Pain is unavoidable in this fallen world. You will be hurt, wronged, and offended by others. There's no way around it"* (p. 40). What are the implications of this reality? How could keeping this fact in mind be helpful?

2. *"The outcome of our lives is not determined by what happens to us but by how we respond to what happens to us"* (p. 41).

It's been said that we live in a culture that celebrates "victimhood." What are some of the consequences of that way of thinking? Can you think of an instance in which you have been tempted to think of yourself as a "victim" of your circumstances or of others' choices, rather than assuming responsibility for your own responses? How could the statement above be liberating?

3. Nancy explains that *"there are essentially two ways of responding to life's hurts and unfair experiences"* (p. 42). Discuss those two different responses and their outcomes. Ask one or more in the group to share about a time when they responded as a "debt collector."

4. If Mr. Ashmore had successfully sued the hospital, do you think that legal victory would have brought him peace and satisfaction? How does our legal system sometimes promote unforgiveness? Is it ever right to sue another party for negligence or wrongdoing? What biblical principles should guide that decision?

5. Rudy Tomjanovich said that hating the player who had ruined his career would be *"like taking poison and hoping someone else would die"* (p. 49). What did he mean? How is bitterness like poison? How does it affect us and others?

6. Close your time by providing an opportunity for group members to share one or more of their responses to the "Making It Personal" questions on page 52.

On Your Own

Read Matthew 18:21–35 prayerfully. What makes "debt collecting" so unthinkable for those who are in the Kingdom of

God? Are you a debt collector? Ask the Lord to speak to you through this passage about any debts you may be holding over an offender's head.

Grace Note

"Whenever you standing praying, if you have anything against anyone, forgive him" (Mark 11:25 NKJV). We are sinful. How can we know that our prayers will be accepted by a holy God? He is a *just* God. He does not whitewash sin. Our sins deeply offend Him. God cannot let sin go unpunished. Jesus paid for our sins so we can boldly approach the throne of grace. Our ability to forgive others is based on that divine exchange. Mindful of how much we've been forgiven, we can forgive others and trust our heavenly Father that justice will be done.

Chapter Two:
WHAT HAPPENS WHEN WE REFUSE

Getting Started

Bitterness is such a subtle sin. We are usually the ones most blind to our own bitterness. In light of this session's topic, start this meeting with prayer, asking the Holy Spirit to shine His spotlight on any hidden roots of bitterness that may be "buried" in your heart and mind.

Read Hebrews 12:1–17, having each group member read one or more verses alternately. What insights in this passage can help us deal with the "hard things" that come into our lives?

Going Deeper

1. It can be difficult to detect (or acknowledge) bitterness in our hearts. What are some of the telltale evidences that hurt may have turned to bitterness in someone's life?

2. What are some of the actions and attitudes that often accompany bitterness? (See Ephesians 4:31–32; Romans 3:14; Colossians 3:19.)

3. Discuss how bitterness affects us in each of the following areas:

- Our mind and emotions
- Our relationships with others
- Our relationship with God

4. Share any insights that stand out to you from the parable of the unforgiving servant (Matthew 18:21–35).

What perspective does the extraordinary amount of money owed by the first servant give us in relation to our sin and the forgiveness we have received from God?

Jesus said that when we refuse to forgive, we set ourselves up to be turned over to "tormentors" (v. 34 KJV). What could some of those tormentors be?

How does a failure to forgive affect our capacity to experience God's love and forgiveness (v. 35)?

5. How does unforgiveness open the door for Satan to gain a foothold in our lives?

6. Nancy says she is convinced that *"sexual sin is almost invariably linked to a root of bitterness, as are many other sins and issues"* (p. 75). Discuss how sexual sin can be the fruit of a root of bitterness.

7. Provide an opportunity for group members to share what God showed them through one or more of the "Making It Personal" questions on page 81.

Take time to pray for any who express a desire to receive God's grace to deal with a root of bitterness in their heart.

On Your Own

With your spouse or a friend of the same sex, review the statements revealing bitterness on page 58. Ask this individual if he or she sees any evidence of unforgiveness in your life in these areas. If any issues surface, pray together for the grace to release all your debtors, on the basis of what Jesus has done for you.

Grace Note

If you find yourself tempted by condemnation and discouragement, remember that these reactions are evidence of pride still lurking within. Instead, acknowledge that you don't have the ability to forgive in your own strength. Exercise faith that God can give you the grace to put away all bitterness, just as He gives you the grace to repent from other sins. The more you need God's grace, the more you magnify Him!

Chapter Three:
THE PROMISE OF FORGIVENESS

Getting Started

Corrie ten Boom said: *"It is not on our forgiveness, any more than on our own goodness, that the world's healing hinges, but on His"* (p. 90). Are you familiar with this Holocaust survivor? (Her powerful story has been recounted in a book and a feature film, both titled *The Hiding Place*.) What do you remember about how Corrie's life illustrates the message of choosing forgiveness?

In what sense does the world's healing hinge on the forgiveness of Christ?

Since Last Time

How did it go with your spouse/accountability partner as you reviewed the statements that could reveal bitterness? Did they share any observations about bitterness that had previously gone unnoticed by you?

Going Deeper

1. How do the word pictures of a "cancelled note" (p. 82) and the "delete" button on a computer illustrate the nature of forgiveness?

2. What is meant when we say that forgiveness is a promise (pp. 85–86)? What "right" do we relinquish when we forgive someone?

3. What impressed you about the accounts of Ernie Cassutto (pp. 87–89) and/or Lorna Wilkinson (pp. 96–99)? How did their choice to forgive impact their "enemies"?

4. Nancy asks: *"Is there a threshold of pain beyond which we are not required to forgive, one perhaps where it is impossible to forgive?"* (p. 90). How would you answer that question, based on the Word of God?

5. In what sense is forgiveness at the heart of the gospel?

6. How would you respond to the concern that forgiveness lets the offender off the hook from experiencing consequences for his/her sin?

When we forgive someone, does that mean that person should not be held accountable and experience consequences for his/her wrong choices? Discuss the fact that forgiveness and justice are not mutually exclusive.

7. What do the biblical accounts of Joseph and Abigail teach us about responding to those who have sinned against us?

8. Allow time for group members who wish to do so to share one or more of their responses to the "Making It Personal" questions on page 101.

On Your Own

Perhaps like Ernie Cassutto, your forgiveness could lead to someone receiving God's mercy for their sins against Him. Does any specific situation come to mind? Begin to pray for God's gracious intervention in this person's.

Grace Note

If you fear forgiving someone because of the seriousness of the offense, remember that your heavenly Father hates that sin more than you ever could. He will not let it go unpunished. Like your own sins, this offense can be redeemed by the merciful atoning work of the cross of Christ.

Chapter Four:
FORGIVING FOR JESUS' SAKE

Getting Started

This chapter is the heart of the book. Start this meeting focusing on the love and mercy of God as seen in the sacrifice of Christ on the cross. You may want to read selected verses, offer brief prayers of thanksgiving and worship, or lead out in singing an appropriate hymn or chorus.

Going Deeper

1. What does Oswald Chambers mean when he says, *"The only ground on which God can forgive me is the Cross of my Lord"* (p. 105)? What are the implications of the Cross for those who have been wronged? How does the Cross make it possible for us to extend forgiveness to others?

2. In this chapter Nancy talks about how the most difficult ordeals we suffer can be used by God for redemptive purposes in our lives. What are some biblical passages or examples that bear out this point?

3. Who are the three characters in the book of Philemon and what are the three roles they represent in broken relationships? What do they teach us about the nature and goal of forgiveness?

Can you think of a contemporary example of a "peacemaker" —someone you know or have heard about who has sought to bring about reconciliation between two individuals or parties?

4. Have you heard people say, "I just can't forgive myself for what I've done"? Perhaps you've thought this yourself. How does that concept line up with God's Word? How would you minister to someone who says she is struggling to "forgive herself"?

5. When she saw the deep-seated anger and bitterness in his heart, Judah Ben Hur's friend Esther said to him, *"You seem to be now the very thing you set out to destroy, giving evil for evil. Hatred is turning you to stone . . . It's as though you had become Messala* [the friend who had betrayed him to the Romans and who was the object of his drive for vengeance]" (p. 119). Do you think it is an accurate observation that we often become like those we most resent? Why might that be true?

6. *"There is no more credible evidence to the world that the gospel we proclaim is real than when we extend His forgiveness to others"* (p. 117). How does our willingness or our refusal to forgive impact the way unbelievers view the gospel? What are some real-life examples (negative or positive) you have witnessed, experienced, or heard about?

7. Explain the meaning of the phrase, "forgiveness in, forgiveness out."

8. Take time for group members to share one or more of their responses to the "Making It Personal" questions on page 121.

On Your Own

Read Romans 8:12–39. As you do, consider any areas in which you have been wronged and are struggling to forgive. Make a list of statements and promises in this passage that have bearing on your situation.

Grace Note

It may have been a surprise to you to find out that you don't need to forgive yourself—you need to receive God's forgiveness. But walking in assurance of that forgiveness is the best way to combat the common temptations of condemnation and regret. Even better: this is not something you have to do in your own strength. You don't have to gut it out or psych yourself up with motivational speeches. You just need to humble yourself to agree with God's view of your sin and your need to receive His lavish mercy.

Chapter Five:
THE ART OF
FORGIVENESS

Getting Started

With this chapter, we take a slight turn in our journey of forgiveness. We've spent time explaining the "why" of forgiveness; now we will focus on the "how." We'll consider how the process of forgiveness takes place and how we can greater intimacy with God and freedom in our relationships.

Since Last Time

How did you apply Romans 8:12–39 to a situation you are facing? What insights did the Lord show you from that passage?

Going Deeper

1. The quote at the beginning of this chapter reads, *"The glory of Christianity is to conquer by forgiveness."* What do you think the author meant by that statement? Can you think of an illustration (biblical or contemporary) of this principle?

2. Review the three practical steps to forgiving others that Nancy outlined in this chapter (pp. 127–35). Discuss why each step is important and some of the barriers that may be encountered in the process of taking that step.

3. Why is "forgetting" the offense not a requirement of true forgiveness?

4. What if the offender is 95 percent wrong in the hurtful circumstance and you are only 5 percent wrong? How does God want you to respond?

5. Discuss the role of feelings and faith in forgiving others.

6. What does Nancy mean when she says "forgiveness is supernatural" (p. 142)? What are the implications of that reality?

7. What insights into forgiveness can we glean from Gracia Burnham's testimony (pp. 135–38)?

8. What struck you about the account of Nancy's friend whose husband committed adultery (pp. 139–41)? How can someone who has been wronged so grievously come to view their experience as "a gift to embrace" (p. 140)?

On Your Own

If you haven't already done so, make sure to fill out a "pathway of forgiveness" sheet as recommended in this chapter. Bring it to discuss the next time.

Grace Note

"Now that you know these things, you will be blessed if you do them" (John 13:17 NIV). Blessing comes through believing and putting that belief into action. Conversely, neglecting or refusing to obey means forfeiting God's blessing!

Chapter Six:
ANGRY AT GOD

Getting Started

"Whatever men expect, they soon come to think they have a right to; the sense of disappointment can, with very little skill on our part, be turned into a sense of injury" (C.S. Lewis, p. 146).

What are some examples in our culture (or current events) of unfulfilled expectations and disappointment turning into anger and a "sense of injury"?

Since Last Time

What did your "pathway to forgiveness" sheets look like? Were you surprised by anything that took place as you filled them out? How did you experience the grace to obey?

Warming Up

Were you amused by the frivolous lawsuit filed by Donald Drusky? What made his claims so outrageous?

Going Deeper

1. Why do you think there is so much anger being expressed in our day?

2. How would you respond to the question Nancy raises on page 149: *"Do we ever have the right to be angry at God?"*

Biblical authors sometimes ask God "tough" questions and express intense feelings to Him about their suffering. Talk about when "being honest with God" about our pain crosses the line and becomes a sinful response.

3. *"I have come to believe that, at one level, all bitterness is ultimately directed toward God"* (pp. 152–53). Discuss how this could be true, even in a situation where someone has been wronged by another individual and is not consciously bitter toward God.

4. How did Bill Elliff's mother's response to her husband's adultery illustrate the grace of God and the power of forgiveness?

5. What is wrong with the notion that sometimes we need to forgive God?

6. What does the biblical account of Naomi reveal about the causes and consequences of bitterness?

7. What does John Piper's response to his cancer diagnosis reveal about his view of God (pp. 160–61)? How does his perspective differ from the view of God expressed by Naomi in the book of Ruth?

How does our view of God and His providence affect our capacity to respond to God in the midst of pain and to forgive those who wrong us?

8. Take time to discuss any personal responses you feel free to share from the Making It Personal questions on page 168.

For Next Time

"Listen to yourself. What are you saying about Him? What is your life communicating to others about Him?" (p. 160). Between now and the next time your group meets, ask your spouse, your children, a colleague, roommate, or accountability partner (any or all) to help you listen to yourself. Ask them to gently (but honestly!) reflect back to you what your response to challenging circumstances communicates about God. Make a note of those observations and come back prepared to share what you've learned.

Grace Note

The fruit of doing the hard "heart work" of forgiveness truly is the sweet restoration of everything you've prayed for. It might *feel* like God is getting you to buckle under His will, but truly there is a sweet reward in trusting God for the final resolution of your circumstances!

Chapter Seven:
WHAT TRUE FORGIVENESS IS —AND ISN'T

Getting Started

In this session, we will discuss the hard truth that there is simply no comfort in forgiveness. That's because, as John Piper so eloquently reminds us, *"God gave His own Son to suffer more than we could ever make anyone suffer for what they have done to us"* (p. 170).

Since Last Time

What did people report to you about how your response to adversity reflects on God? Were you surprised? Encouraged? Convicted?

Going Deeper

1. Review the four myths about forgiveness that Nancy addresses in this chapter. Give group members an opportunity to share which if any of these myths they have struggled with at some point in their journey.

2. Is it possible to forgive someone and still experience random emotions that seemingly contradict forgiveness? How should those emotions be viewed and handled?

3. Why might God choose not to allow us to forget an offense, even after we have chosen to forgive the offender? How does God desire for us to use the memory of our pain and hurt? (See 2 Corinthians 1:3–5). Can one or more in your group illustrate this principle out of their personal experience?

4. Discuss the relationship between the *point* of forgiveness and the *process* of healing and restoration.

5. What three good "habits" does Nancy point out that Paul exercised throughout his life (pp. 181–83)?

6. Talk about the quality of "forbearance." What does it mean? Why is it important? Have group members share some practical, personal illustrations of current or recent situations in their lives where they need(ed) to exercise forbearance.

7. What are some take-aways that spoke to you from the story of Steve Saint, whose missionary father was murdered in the jungles of Ecuador more than fifty years ago? Describe the spiritual legacy Steve's widowed mother left for her son and the impact her response to the loss of her husband had on him years later as a grown man.

Discuss the kind of legacy you want to leave for the next generation in relation to forgiveness.

For Next Time

Think of two practical ways you can show forbearance in your home in the coming days. How can you show forbearance in situations you face at work or church? Plan ahead for certain temptations you can expect to face and be prepared to extend grace!

Grace Note

Remembering those times we've been forgiven will make us more thankful; it will also make us more compassionate toward the failings and weaknesses of others. Meditate on the quote from John Piper at the beginning of this chapter (p. 170). An understanding of Jesus' sacrifice for you—enabling you to forgive—will help you to respond to hurtful people and circumstances in His grace.

Chapter Eight:
RETURNING A BLESSING

Getting Started

When you picked up this book, you may have thought the most challenging part would be to extend genuine forgiveness. Now, in this final chapter, we explore the final step—a step that is impossible apart from the Holy Spirit's work in our lives. Start this session in prayer, petitioning Him for the grace we need to be truly Christ-like.

Since Last Time

How did you do with "Project Forbearance"?

Warming Up

Romans 12 is the backbone for this chapter. Read through the chapter together, taking turns reading one or more verses. What is the "big idea" of this chapter?

Going Deeper

1. Have you ever known someone who seemed to be "stuck emotionally" in the pain of their past, even after making the choice to forgive those who wronged them? What is the "key" Nancy addresses in this chapter that can help people move forward in peace and freedom? Reread Romans 12:19–21, where this principle is clearly stated.

2. *"Forgiveness requires that we go 'above and beyond' just releasing our offenders"* (p. 195). Describe what "above and beyond" might look like or include.

How can we "overcome evil with good"? How did Martin Burnham demonstrate this principle (p. 198)? How is this concept illustrated in the life of Joseph (p. 202)?

3. Share with the group how you responded to the Making It Personal exercise on page 209. (Be as transparent as possible, while being careful not to reflect negatively on others as you do.)

4. *"God has never met a circumstance so dreadful that it can't be recast into a trophy of His mercy and grace"* (p. 199). What difference would it make in our responses to painful circumstances if we really believed that?

5. Read 1 Peter 2:19–25. How can we become instruments of God's redemptive grace in the lives of those who have sinned against us, as we forgive and bless them? Can you think of an instance where you have seen this take place?

On Your Own

Luke 6:27–28 tells us to love our enemies, do good to those who hate us, bless those who curse us, and pray for those who abuse us. In the coming days, be intentional about praying for someone who is opposed to you or has mistreated you. Then seek ways to fulfill the rest of this passage as wisdom and discretion dictate. One suggestion: You may need to discuss this with a mature believer or accountability partner, someone who will pray for you, help you take the next steps wisely, and also follow up to make sure you've done what you planned.

Grace Note

As you do this assignment and the Holy Spirit shows you ways to bless your offender, you may still struggle with being a "channel of blessing." Remember that God supplies the grace we need to fulfill His commands. Through Christ's strength and grace, you *can* overcome evil with good. If pride stands in the way, pray that God will give you a broken, tender heart. Your heavenly Father wants you to experience fully the freedom of forgiveness.

Afterword:
THE POWER OF FORGIVENESS

Getting Started

The quote from Elisabeth Elliot at the beginning of this chapter ends with these words: *"Who can stand up to the force of forgiveness?"* There is immense power in forgiveness—power to accomplish much more than just our own freedom and release from bitterness.

Since Last Time

Did you have an opportunity to pray for and show kindness to someone who opposes you or has sinned against you? Have you seen any fruit of your obedience—in you or in them?

Final Questions

1. This chapter highlighted the power of forgiveness. How can forgiveness bring healing into the life of the *offender?* What about in the life of the *offended?* How can forgiveness impact *future* situations, relationships, and generations?

2. For years, Bonnie played and replayed a "record" in her mind of her mother's angry outbursts and behavior. One day Bonnie was challenged to "break the record" of those past wrongs. What was the result when she did?

Is there a "record" you have been needing to break? Share with the group what God has been saying to you and take time to pray for those who express a need for prayer.

3. What is the ultimate goal of forgiveness (p. 216)? How is God's glory put on display when we choose forgiveness?

4. At first blush, the Cross seemed to be a colossal defeat for God's program. How did it prove to be His ultimate victory? What are the implications of the triumph of the Cross for our lives in this fallen world?

5. What have you learned from this study on forgiveness that has been most helpful, enlightening, or impacting to you?

6. Since this study began, what changes have you experienced in your life, your relationship with the Lord, or your relationships with others?

Grace Note

What better way to end a study on forgiveness than to spend some time in worship, joining in the heavenly celebration of the redeemed around the throne.

Then I saw a new heaven and a new earth, for the first heaven and the first earth had passed away, and there was no longer any sea. I saw the Holy City, the new Jerusalem, coming down out of heaven from God, prepared as a bride beautifully dressed for her husband. And I heard a loud voice from the throne saying, "Now the dwelling of God is with men, and he will live with them. They will be his people, and God himself will be with them and be their God. He will wipe every tear from their eyes. There will be no more death or mourning or crying or pain, for the old order of things has passed away." He who was seated on the throne said, "I am making everything new!" (Revelation 21:1–5)